The Heart of a Woman

Reclaim, Release and Renew

Shaneka L. McClarty

The Heart of a Woman
Reclaim, Release and Renew
Published by Shaneka L. McClarty

© 2013 by Shaneka L. McClarty
ISBN 13: 978-0615962788
ISBN 10: 0615962785

Cover design by: Liedtke Design
Cover image is owned by: Shaneka L. McClarty

Unless otherwise indicated, Scripture quotations are from:
New American Standard Bible ® (NASB)
© 1960, 1977, 1995 by the Lockman Foundation.
Used by permission

For my three Princesses.

CONTENTS

INTRODUCTION

How many times have you fallen in love? How many times have you surrendered your heart to someone and had it broken? Falling in love is a beautiful thing but no one wants to experience the pain of a heart break no matter how inevitable it may be. After a bad break-up, you may have long nights of crying only to awake with swollen eyes the next morning. Or maybe you had difficulty concentrating at work because you were thinking about the person who hurt you. You probably felt depressed with a lack of interest to do the things you normally would enjoy doing. In fact, you didn't have the desire to get up and leave your house because you would have rather stayed in bed to sleep. Then there are the moments where you may have eaten delicious foods to comfort yourself only to rediscover your emptiness at the bottom of the plate or bowl. Nevertheless, it seems like you could see your ex, hear him and, in some cases, feel him. You wondered what he was doing and who he was doing it with. It hurt so badly until it made you sick. Heart break sucks!

When a woman loves, she loves hard and deeply. It's the experiences from a heart break that teaches her to guard and protect her heart and it is at that moment a woman learns to love out of fear. Fear of not being enough, fear of being left alone or fear of rejection. Often times the fear keeps her in the relationship due to the desperate chase and longing for the love that she experienced in the beginning. A woman's spiritual challenge is to honor herself based on the principles of truth, respect and self-love. She must reclaim her power from the man that dishonors her heart; release the hurt and pain from broken relationships and lies; and renew her mind to receive the blessings her Higher Power has released into the universe for her to receive. The path to this type of freedom and empowerment can be difficult for most women because they do not know where to start or how to let go. Nevertheless, I believe our Higher Power gives us the same lesson over and over until we master it. So when it comes to the matters of the heart, you must examine what lesson there is for you to learn and consider the relationship or the man as the teacher.

I wrote this book to reach more women who have been heart broken and struggling with the healing process. I want to help you to identify the lesson, heal and move on. Although the premise of this book does not represent all women, it may represent you or someone you know. This book is for the woman who is ready to make a drastic change in her life- no more drama, no more fear and no more heart breaks. It is for the woman who is ready for authentic, respectful and faithful love. This journey from heart break to wholeness is not a sprint race. I want you to read this book slowly. Take your time to absorb the information and reflect on the questions that are presented to you. Open up your bible and read the scriptures that are suggested and meditate on the scriptures to apply them in your life.

The beauty of a relationship is the intimate, emotional connection that happens when you allow someone to connect with your heart and soul. I want to connect with you as if you were sitting in my office on my couch. Get a journal to write in while you are reading this book as it is designed to encourage you to open up about your past, present and future. Throughout the book, I share insightful stories about people I have met who have checked out of the heart-break hotel and moved into the penthouse of self-love.

Lastly, there are many good self-help books on the market to help you think like a man, learn smart dating tactics, and how to shop for a husband. I am not offering dating advice; I am providing a small gift of wisdom about life. There is truth in every tragedy, so I want you to be open-minded and open your heart to what your Higher Power has been trying to teach you. Always ask yourself, "What lesson in this experience do I need to learn?" Whenever you start to approach life in this manner, you accept life as your University and the people who come into your world as the teachers.

Each painful experience or heart break changes who you are as a person. The experience is like clay taking part in molding who you are. Most importantly, it's not the experience that defines you; instead it is how you respond to the painful experience. This is the spiritual challenge in life; either resist the lesson and prolong it or embrace it and grow. Nevertheless, each lesson you master within your heart will bring you closer to your purpose.

RECLAIM AND REST

1
HEART SURGERY

Whenever you fall in love, you surrender a part of yourself to what feels good to you. There is nothing wrong with the process of falling in love because love is a beautiful thing. When a woman surrenders her heart, she is basically saying, "I like you and I trust you." She is also saying, "I want more of this good feeling." What changes all of this and what breaks a woman's heart? A lot of things; but the major indicators are lies, infidelity, and abuse. Shockingly, a woman may add more pain to her heart break by holding on to the relationship because she does not want to let go of how good the "falling in love" part felt to her.

Interestingly, I have learned that God will use your pain for a purpose. You may not understand it right now and it may not feel like there is a greater purpose in it, but there is. In my private practice I am most passionate about building hope in people. I would not say that I am a relationship builder because I do not have the power to build your relationship; only you have the power to do that. I, on the other hand, have the power to teach, guide and support you. Nevertheless, I enjoy building people up by letting them know how important they are and how special their lives are. I am a hope-builder. When you have hope you believe and you fight. When you have hope you thrive and you succeed. With hope there is faith.

Eight years ago, I met a young lady who was deeply hurt. She carried around a lot of wounds from a four-year relationship. The goal was to help her to grasp that even though she was hurt; she was not broken and even if she felt broken; she was not shattered. Each time I sat with her for a counseling session, it was like sitting in a dark hole. The energy was so dreary, hopeless, defeated and heavy whereby I felt emotionally drained at times. Can you imagine how this young woman felt everyday of her life?

Whenever you search for something in a relationship to meet an unmet need in your heart you are ultimately searching for trouble. Can a man really make you feel valued when you do not value yourself? Can he make you feel secure when you feel insecure? Does he have the power to change your self-esteem and make you love yourself? To some extent women have used having a man as a safety blanket. A man can make you feel good about yourself, but not completely. The power to do any of this lies within you and you can do it. There is hope because the light is not at the end of the tunnel; the light is within you. It may be a small glimmer of light, but at least it is there. Even if, within your heart, you feel there is darkness and pain know that the possibility of hope and light is still there because the only power darkness has is to conceal. Consequently, a symbolic heart surgery is not about concealing or covering up your pain. Instead, it is about exposing your pain, staring it dead in the eyes, accepting the lesson it has for you, and releasing it. So where does a woman with a broken heart go from here?

One of my favorite soul-searching questions I like to ask in counseling sessions is, "Who are you?" Sometimes people tell me they do not know. Other times my clients will give me a list of positive adjectives to describe their appearance or accomplishments. Then I encourage them to share with me the person that no one sees; the person they do not reveal to others. Silence lingers in the room for a moment as the client thinks about the statement and they either provide an answer that is derived from fear or truth. I understand it is very difficult for most people to be vulnerable and transparent with someone, especially if there is a fear of being judged, hurt or rejected. Personal growth comes from a level of vulnerability within our ability to surrender that guides us to become better human beings. Whenever your mind and heart connects, the process of spiritual awakening begins which leads to a wonderful life of happiness and freedom. To get started on this journey to freedom and happiness within your heart, you must prepare yourself for heart surgery.

Before a heart surgery, the doctor presents a list of things for the patient to do or not do. Normally, the patient is not to eat or drink 24 hours before the surgery, they are instructed to get a good night's rest, arrive to the hospital a few hours before the procedure to complete registration paperwork and provide information about their medical history and medications. After the surgery is complete, the doctor informs the patient of the post-surgery rules for recovery.

In this book, a heart attack symbolically represents the painful experiences you have endured in relationships such as lies, infidelity, betrayal, manipulation, abuse and rejection. When you make the choice to position your heart for healing, you are making a decision to symbolically undergo open heart surgery. In other words, you will undergo multiple CAT scans, MRIs and X-rays of your heart to examine the core issues of unresolved pain. You will identify the blocked arteries as a result of your power and energy being taken from you, irregular heartbeats that were caused by multiple lies and disappointments, as well as heart attacks that were brought on by torn relationships. There is only one pre-surgical procedure required before we begin. You will need to prepare for heart surgery by making a choice. You or him? It is impossible for you to heal while holding on to an unhealthy relationship because it is bad for your heart.

Heart attacks normally occur in unhealthy relationships. A healthy relationship requires both parties to be selfless. In an unhealthy relationship there is selfishness which means the needs of one or both parties will not be met. Think about your past unsuccessful relationships. What selfish acts do you recall taking part in? What selfish acts did you witness in your partner? Your lists are very important, in that it will become a self-inventory of correction for you as well as an assessment of red flags to be aware of in future relationships. Women in unhealthy relationships make their decisions out of fear. There is fear of being rejected, fear of letting him go and he becomes a "good man" for the next woman or fear of being alone.

The sacrifice that a woman makes to remain in a relationship where she does not feel valued, loved and respected is a fearful act which depletes her self-worth. This continued act of selfless sacrifice, on your part, can be taken for granted over time and you may be perceived as weak or naïve. At some point you will start to lose yourself and you will not want to honor the man or the relationship if you are not honored. Putting a man first while sacrificing your needs, happiness and desires only decreases your power. Be aware that moving forward, I will challenge you to make several important decisions and whenever you make a decision you have two choices-Fear or Faith. I am encouraging you to make a choice right now. Who will you passionately love, respect and honor- You or him?

Choosing to put yourself first is not a selfish act because authentic love comes from your ability to love yourself. If you are in an unhealthy relationship right now, you can choose to continue doing what you are doing or choose to do something different. Once you make the decision to choose yourself it becomes an act of empowerment. It is a decision you make out of faith and not fear. At that moment, your decision can be interpreted as a declaration to healing.

Who are you at the core of your heart? How much of yourself have you given away? How many men, women, family or friends have hurt you? How long will you hide behind your shadow with fear of loving and trusting again? Sometimes the pain hurts so bad you feel like you want to die, but fortunately, dying is not an option because your life is priceless. Just make your decision right now about what you will do with your pain. Will you choose yourself or the person who hurt you?

After you make the choice to choose yourself, then you must complete a checklist of symptoms or "heart defects." Experiences in life, good or bad, changes who you are. It is impossible not to be affected or influenced by your experiences. If someone poured kind words into you and affirmed you, it affected your life for the better. On the other hand, if someone ridiculed you or was unsupportive of you, then it surely affected you as well. During this process, the focus is not on the men who hurt you; the focus is on you. This is where you begin to examine your root issues. I will use the tree analogy to explain how we will examine your root issues. Look at yourself symbolically as a tree. What you choose to show people are the branches and leaves of the tree which may be how fashionable and beautiful you are, intelligent, dedicated or funny. In comparison, the roots of the tree is what people cannot see. You know the roots are there but its hidden deep beneath the earth's soil similar to how you may be hiding or camouflaging your heart defects. Search within your heart and be honest with yourself about who you are, how you present yourself in a relationship, and who you have become.

Complete the checklist below to identify your heart defects as a result of the heart attacks you have experienced.

Fearful	_Demanding
_of change	_Overly sacrificing
_of rejection	_Possessive
_of abandonment	_Poor communicator
_of failure	_Poor listener
_of being alone	_Bitter
_of being hurt	_Withdrawn
_of intimacy	_Guarded
_of financial instability	_Low self-esteem
_Materialistic	_Unreliable
_Excessively sensitive	_Poor boundaries
_Seductive	_Passive
_Manipulative	_Poor self-discipline
_Emotionally dependent	_Liar
_Aggressive	_Cheater
_Controlling	_Instigator
_Arrogant	_Gossiper
_Stubborn	_Envious
_Jealous	

Heart Notes

- ♥ Describe what you like about falling in love.
- ♥ So far you have to make a decision- you or him?
- ♥ Do you have the courage to choose yourself?
- ♥ When you make a decision, you have two choices- Fear or Faith.
- ♥ Think about the events that led to your heart break(s). What heart defects did you develop as a result?
- ♥ Your pain can do two things: lead you to God or away from Him.
- ♥ What will you do with your pain?
- ♥ What scares you the most about heart break?

Scriptures

Search me, O God, and know my heart; try me and know my anxious thoughts. Psalm 139:23

And He who sits on the throne said, "Behold, I am making all things new. Revelation 21:5

Then you will call, and the Lord will answer; you will cry, and He will say, "Here I am." Isaiah 58:9

He heals the brokenhearted and binds up their wounds. Psalm 147:3

2
EMOTIONAL BAGGAGE

After you have identified the root issues or your heart defects, it may not be easy to admit or accept who you are at the core of your heart. You have some baggage that you have been unpacking in each relationship whether you want to admit it or not and your emotional baggage has been projected onto each man. The sultry singer, Erykah Badu, melodically sang in her song, '*Bag Lady*,' that a woman would hurt her back carrying around bags like that. The lyrics continued to say, "One day, he gonna say you crowdin my space.... so pack light." How do you begin to emotionally pack light?

A man cannot be responsible (and does not want to be responsible) for carrying or cleaning up your emotional baggage. He may not have the patience to stay around to deal with it. Emotional baggage can be described as difficulty trusting, self-esteem issues, low self-worth, abandonment issues, unresolved grief or unresolved hurt. A woman with emotional baggage may use her body sexually to receive love, may be highly sensitive and suspicious of a man cheating, questions a man's whereabouts, is doubtful of what a man says, sneaks into a man's personal belongings (cell phone/email) or stalk a man. Some women may feel nothing is wrong with doing any of these things; however it's the motive behind the action that is important. Is it done out of fear? If so, then there is an issue.

A long time ago, I met a young woman who noted that she never had a relationship with her mother who was the local drug addict and prostitute. She knew who her mother was; however her mother never wanted anything to do with her. This young lady stated this made her feel invisible. As a child, she excelled in many things to receive her mother's approval but to her dismay her mother continued to reject and ignore her even after years of being clean. She grew up with a scarlet letter as everyone in her town knew her mother had abandoned her. This was difficult for her as a child because she didn't understand why. As an adult, she worked hard to be recognized in life by achieving many accomplishments in her career. Unfortunately, she was not successful in relationships with men or women. On the outside, she presented a strong, dominating personality. She over-talked people and appeared to be in control.

She was determined to be seen and heard; however her behavior pushed people away. With men, she moved too fast because after six months she started to talk about getting married and having kids. She wanted to make sure she locked the man down so that he would not leave her. Unfortunately, the men in her life would not commit. Sadly, she was perceived as a bitch by women because she was determined to never let another woman make her feel invisible like her mother did. She gossiped about other women and was always in a competition with them. She had no clue how to be a friend because she did not trust anyone. The young lady's heart defects were fear of abandonment, insecurities about not being good enough, and controlling out of fear of rejection. This is the emotional baggage she unpacked in her relationships and friendships.

Now take a hard look at yourself. Really pay attention to your heart and listen to what it has been holding in for you. Unpack your emotional baggage and decide what you will keep and what you will let go of.

Let Go

When God created woman, I believe he gave her a very special gift to use that I call an internal compass. You may call your internal compass your gut or intuition but it's a priceless gift to have. Unfortunately, women often underestimate the power of their internal compass by second-guessing the messages they receive. The best advice is to always listen to what your internal compass tells you because if it does not feel right then it is not right for you. As a woman, you always know when it is time to walk away; however the difficult part is letting go. Furthermore, it is not healthy for you to stay in a relationship that is not compatible with your emotional needs. Sacrificing your needs for the sake of a man is called sabotage. Who wants to sabotage their life on purpose? No one does; not even you.

A young lady came to see me for counseling and had a tremendous amount of guilt and shame because the man she had given herself to had left her. Even though she was in so much pain, I felt this was for the best. During the relationship, she ignored the red flags because she didn't have the courage to let him go so it appears the universe arranged for the break up to happen. In the end, this man had given her a gift that she did not want, neither did she ask for. In fact, this type of gift she could never get rid of because there was no cure or pill to make it go away. She had every reason to feel hurt and ashamed; however she had no idea that her actions, which were done out of fear, would sabotage her life. When she had the opportunity to leave him she became afraid. She stated she needed proof of his infidelity. I recalled asking her, "If you had proof would you really let him go or would you compromise yourself?" At that time, she did not have an answer to my question except for needing proof before walking away. Unfortunately, she never received the proof she needed because he walked away from her. Fear set her up and now her life has been changed forever.

Whenever you choose to stay rather than leave an unhealthy relationship, you are taking part in sabotaging your life. You are doing that; no one else just you. You are making the decision to re-traumatize yourself, crucify yourself, or in this case, cause your own heart attack. God always gives us a way out of an unhealthy or unsafe situation; however it is up to us to take advantage of the opportunity to get out. The power is transferred from the man to you when you let go and walk away. No man can hurt any woman who is not physically or emotionally available to him. You can begin to reclaim your power by acknowledging what hurt you; not who hurt you. It's the act that hurt you; not the person. Cheating hurts. Lying hurts. Abuse and rejection hurt. Whenever you see the warning signs do not ignore them. Acknowledge the emotional violation and watch where you displace your power- to the act or the man.

I say all of this because many times women look at the man and say, "He hurt me." To an extent this is true; however it was his actions or words that hurt you. If three men cheated on you, then being betrayed hurt you. It's the lies and deception you do not like even though the message was delivered by and through three different men.

Heart Notes

- ♥ Who hurt you physically as a child? Teenager? Adult?
- ♥ The emotional baggage I carry from these heart attacks are___.
- ♥ Who tore down your self-esteem as a child? Teenager? Adult?
- ♥ What were the negative, hurtful statements people said to you?
- ♥ Which negative statements have you etched into your heart and carry around today?
- ♥ Describe the behaviors you exhibit in a relationship as a result of your emotional baggage.
- ♥ Who do people say you are?
- ♥ Describe what you do not reveal to others?
- ♥ What makes you insecure?
- ♥ Who makes you feel insecure?
- ♥ What do you want in a relationship?
- ♥ What do you need in a relationship?
- ♥ Regardless of how bad the relationship was, what did the man give to you that made you feel special?
- ♥ Look at your list above, are you giving those things to yourself? Why or Why not?
- ♥ What strengths and weaknesses were revealed to you about yourself from these painful relationships?
- ♥ It has been difficult for me to let go of _____ and walk away because _____.
- ♥ The consequences of me staying in the relationship with _____ was _____.
- ♥ When I refused to let go, _____ happened.
- ♥ The lesson I learned was _____.

Scriptures

Create in me a clean heart, O God, and renew a steadfast spirit within me. Psalm 51:10

...the Lord searches all hearts and understands every intent of the thoughts... 1 Chronicles 28:9

Anxiety in a man's heart weighs it down, but a good word makes it glad. Proverbs 12:25

...He restores my soul... Psalm 23:3

I sought the Lord, and He answered me, and delivered me from all my fears. Psalm 34:4

3
EMOTIONAL BOUNDARIES

A few years ago I received an email through my website from a potential client. She basically shared her life story in what appeared to be a three page email. After meeting with her, I could see how talented and caring she was but she was also exhausted from the dating games. She was hurt badly after discovering the man she was dating and loved for a year was married. I helped her to identify all of the warning signs in the relationship and she admitted she ignored each one out of fear of losing him. She said she did not want to complain because even though things were not perfect, at least she was not alone. She shared with me that his dishonesty hurt her the most. Once she connected and listened to her heart, her internal compass revealed it did not matter who was dishonest with her it still hurt. At that moment, she was able to identify one of her emotional boundaries which was dishonesty.

Emotional boundaries are the threshold of your emotions and feelings. For example, if you are feeling like you are taken for granted and not appreciated, you may begin to feel tired and fed up. The emotional boundary is unappreciation. That is the warning sign to pay attention to. Whenever a man makes you feel unappreciated then he has crossed one of your emotional boundaries.

Setting boundaries can protect you from heart attacks. It does not guarantee a man will follow or respect your emotional boundaries, but it will send the message that you are serious, you value yourself and you will not participate in emotional games. When you set emotional boundaries you take control which is an important step towards reclaiming your power and releasing the pain. The boundaries are there for your protection. They help you to recognize what hurts you but you must not compromise when you see the warning signs. In addition, boundaries outline the standards for interacting with you and loving you; they outline the limitations for what you will and will not accept in a relationship. Furthermore, when emotional boundaries are communicated clearly in the beginning of a relationship your partner has the opportunity to understand your limits. Lastly, when your emotional boundaries are violated, your response to his actions show him just how serious you are about your emotional boundaries.

At this time, I want you to begin setting your emotional boundaries. You do this by building a solid foundation using the four principles of a healthy relationship which are Trust, Support, Patience and Respect. These principles, as well as your emotional boundaries, should never be compromised. The four principles are required for any healthy relationship no matter the sex or age. Do not begin any serious relationship without these four principles. Many times women gauge a good relationship based on how they feel which can change. It is very important that the principles are reciprocated and not one-sided. You cannot say, "He trusts me, but I don't trust him" because that is not healthy. Also, you cannot say, "He supports me, but he is not respectful or patient." You must have ALL four principles for stability. There are four legs on a chair and if one leg is wobbly, then the chair is not stable. Imagine if two or three legs on the chair were wobbly then the chair would collapse which is representative of most unhealthy relationships. You would not sit in a wobbly chair, so do not stay in a relationship that has started off rocky. Implementing emotional boundaries is an anthem for your self-worth so apply the four principles to yourself by trusting in you, supporting you, respecting you and being patient with yourself. This is the beginning of an authentic intimacy with yourself.

Emotional Violations

When your emotional boundaries are dishonored then it becomes an emotional violation. Emotional violations are the actions performed against the emotional boundaries. Hint, hint: remember at this stage in your healing process it is the act and not the man. Write that down in your journal because you are one step closer to mastering this lesson you keep getting.

Examples of emotional violations are: abuse, disrespect, infidelity, dishonesty and so on. Whenever there are emotional violations, there should be a consequence. It is the law of the universe; for every action or decision there is a consequence-good or bad. Women have to begin to hold the man accountable by exercising the consequences. This is an act of honoring yourself. You should not compromise or bargain with your emotional boundaries as it should be non-negotiable. Not issuing a consequence for an emotional violation sends the message that what he did (the violation) was okay. It's a level of self-compromise that decreases your power over and over again. For example, how many times has a woman taken a man back after he cheated, lied or disrespected her? It has happened a lot of times. Do not think it won't happen again because it will. Getting mad for a few weeks is not a consequence. Arguing is not a consequence. You have one choice- You or him? Let it go and walk away.

Look at the chart below as a reference to establishing your emotional boundaries. Inside the heart, write the four principles of a healthy relationship. Write your emotional boundaries inside the circles closest to the heart and your emotional violations should be written in the outer circles.

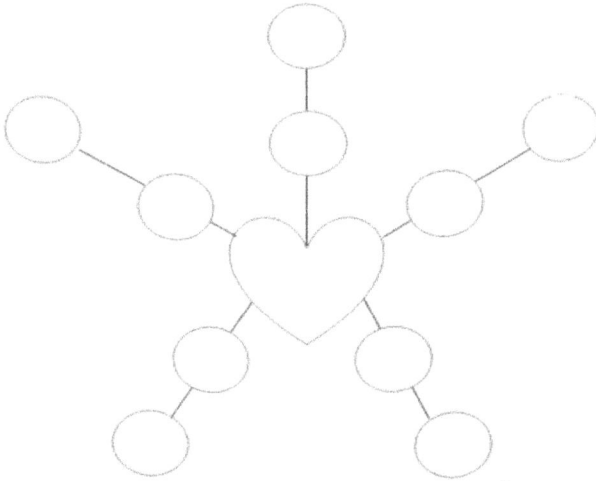

Heart Notes

- ♥ Four principles for a healthy relationship are Trust, Support, Patience and Respect.
- ♥ It is the act or action, not the man.
- ♥ What are your emotional boundaries?
- ♥ What would constitute an emotional violation for you?
- ♥ What consequences will you exercise for each emotional violation?
- ♥ In the past, I have compromised myself for____.
- ♥ What happened when you compromised yourself?
- ♥ Read and meditate on the scriptures below. Reflect on the message in each scripture and how you can apply it to your daily life during this recovery period.
- ♥ Day one: 1 Corinthians 13:4-13
- ♥ Day two: Genesis 31:1-7
- ♥ Day three: Psalm 4:4, 5
- ♥ Day four: Psalm 56:11

Scriptures

Be strong and let your heart take courage, all you who hope in the Lord. Psalm 31:24

He gives strength to the weary, and to him who lacks might He increases power. Isaiah 40:29

Whatsoever things are true, whatever is honorable, whatever is right, whatever is pure, whatever is lovely, whatever is of good repute, if there is any excellence and if anything worthy of praise, dwell on these things. Philippians 4:8

For God did not give us a spirit of timidity, but a spirit of power and love and discipline. 2 Timothy 1:7

RELEASE AND REFLECT

4
RECOVERY PERIOD

Eight years ago, I had major surgery on my left foot. Before I entered the surgical center, my doctor sat down with me in his office and reviewed the post-surgical procedures. He discussed the procedures with me while I was alert and coherent as he knew that after the surgery I would be woozy due to the anesthesia. The doctor provided clear rules for me to follow such as: stay off my feet, elevate my foot when I sat or slept, do not get the bandages wet and take all of my medication as prescribed. He even discussed what would happen to my foot if I did not follow his instructions. Finally, he informed me that the recovery time would be six to eight weeks. After I arrived home, I did just as my doctor had instructed me; however it was very difficult at times because the recovery period was long, painful and uncomfortable.

If you are single or have recently let go and walked away from an unhealthy relationship, then your recovery period has started. You have undergone a symbolic heart surgery as revisiting old wounds can turn into a roller coaster of emotions such as happy, depressed, angry, hurt or worthless. Well, now what do you do? In the meantime, it is important for you to follow the post-surgical recovery procedures which are Rest, Reflect and Prepare.

This is your opportunity to just be still and rest. Give your heart a break; let it heal. Jumping into a new relationship is similar to a drug addict substituting marijuana for cocaine. It's still a drug and it is still unhealthy. The resting phase of your recovery period allows you to hear the voice of your true self. Whether you want to hear her or not, she has a message for you. Your true self has gone through a lot. She has been silenced for too long and now you can give her a platform to speak. Allow your heart to reveal to you what your purpose is and what direction to take. Then step back and begin to reflect on how you were and what kind of woman you truly want to become. Finally, prepare for your future by developing a plan to make your goals happen.

Consider your resting period as a long retreat to honor yourself. Notice I have not suggested the length of your recovery period because it will vary. You cannot rush this process; you must be patient. Notice I just said, 'Patient' which is one of the four principles of a healthy relationship. Get comfortable with patience because it will guide you towards self-control. In the meantime, you will be tempted, but you must resist temptation. It is always the devil's plan to sabotage your life when you are focused. Do not contact your ex no matter how lonely, bored or pain you may feel.

Whenever you are lonely and hurting, you may begin to reminisce and think about the good times. These moments of weakness can lead you to taking the bandages off a fresh wound and allowing your ex to come back into your life. You are stronger than you give yourself credit for, yet I understand that even strong people can be tempted. In the bible, Jesus went into the wilderness to be tempted by the devil (Matthew 4:1). He fasted and prayed for 40 nights and then the devil came to tempt him. Consequently, the devil did not show up immediately instead he waited until Jesus was hungry because he figured Jesus would be weak and desperate. Several times the devil presented Jesus with propositions; however Jesus used the word of God to reject the temptation. Our Lord knew that we would be tempted in life which is one reason why he specifically taught us to pray, "Lead us not into temptation but deliver us from evil" (Matthew 6:13). Instead of turning to your ex or getting a new man to fill the void, use this waiting period in a positive way to honor yourself.

Choose Your Weapon

Since the length of the recovery period is undetermined, you must begin to prepare for the temptation. The key point in the fourth chapter of Matthew that people often miss is the Holy Spirit led Jesus into the wilderness to be tempted. It was a deliberate process for his purpose. You will be tempted and that is a fact; it is a form of distraction to keep you from growing and healing. But temptation can also be a part of the lesson that you must master. In the meantime, what will you use to resist temptation? What is your weapon? To prepare, I suggest you put on the whole armor of self-love to protect and empower yourself. Wear the **belt of truth** around your waist. Let no man lie, woo, entice, seduce, buy or promise his way onto your throne (bed) or into your heart. You are a sacred temple that he cannot afford the price to enter as you are priceless. You must believe that. Second, put on the **breastplate of virtue** to symbolize the respect and honor you have for yourself to guard your heart from corruption. Strap the **stilettoes of peace** on your feet so that you may walk in peace as your steps are choreographed by your Higher Power. It is written that if you keep your mind on God he will keep you in perfect peace (Isaiah 26:3). Accessorize your arms with the **shield of faith.** Have faith in your Higher Power that he will comfort you and provide for you, have faith in your abilities and have faith in your purpose. Adorn your head with the **helmet of liberation** to represent the renewing of your mind and hold on to the **sword of the Spirit** which is the word of God. The word of God is "sharper than any double-edged sword, it penetrates even to dividing soul and spirit, joints and marrow; it judges the thoughts and attitudes of the heart" (Hebrews 4:12).

Start Reflecting

Reflection can be good or bad. It doesn't matter what you are reflecting on; it is how you respond to your reflections. In other words, your reflecting time should be used to examine what lessons are left for you to learn and what you can do differently the next time the same lesson is presented. I remember receiving a text message from a young lady asking me, "How can you despise someone so much and love him at the same time?" I knew the answer to the question; however I wanted her to dig a little deeper so I replied, "I don't know." She then texted me back stating, "This is the sh*t that happens when I haven't had a drink…LOL! Watching him coach our child's team and I'm like how can you be so evil but yet so good with these kids…got my senses though. That's his potential that I see and he doesn't and never will."

Voila! She had the answer inside of her and she didn't need me to give it to her. I decided to help her dig a little deeper so I responded, "Well, that's your answer. You despise how he treats you but you admire his commitment to the kids that he coaches. It's because he is at his best self when he is doing what he loves to do and it is easy for him. No pressure and no judgment from the kids-only acceptance. They listen to him and respect him. He doesn't know how to achieve the same results in an adult relationship, especially with you." The young lady texted back, "Well damn, that sounds about right..." I replied to her saying, "It is the truth and it's his truth except he doesn't know it yet."

This young woman and man have had a roller coaster relationship for more than seven years and during the process conceived a child together. He hurt her so many times until now she despises him. She learned that he is not ready nor is he prepared to be the man she needs him to be. He is emotionally immature and asking him to be responsible, respectful and committed in a grown-up relationship right now is not going to happen. What will happen is a heart attack for her if she lets him back in. The beauty in reflection was not for her to travel down the lane of 'good ole times,' but to look at the spiritual lesson for her to learn. This man is vulnerable and insecure and what she required of him highlighted his insecurities which made him push back harder, scream at her louder and run away from himself. At times, it looked as though he consistently ran away from her but he was really running away from himself. The worst thing that she could have done would be to chase after him because that would spell trouble. In the end, she decided to let him go because she remembered what happened when she stayed in the race with him.

A few months later, she texted me saying, "This year I am focusing on me. I won't have the same mess happen this year like I did last year." I believed her. I truly believed that in her heart she meant what she was saying. It doesn't matter how long it took her to get to the point of choosing herself; it only mattered that she was not just saying those words but her heart was positioned to make it happen. She was entering the preparation stage.

Inside, my heart smiled for her because when a woman makes up her mind and her heart is connected to the decision great things happen. This woman recognized her strength and self-worth and so her healing had begun. She wasn't trying to force this man to be a family with her and their child. She didn't try to change him either. She looked at who he was and accepted it. She looked at his character and his values and accepted that his character and his values were not what she wanted in a partner.

My role in the journey with her was to be supportive and encourage her to stay focused on the commitment she made to herself.

Heart Notes

♥ How can a man tempt you?

♥ When I feel _____ I am tempted to _____ in order to get my needs met. The propositions I have made to a man or am likely to make are _____.

♥ What are your thoughts about taking a temporary break from men to focus on yourself?

♥ What will be your distractions?

♥ Realistically, how long of a recovery period do you need?

♥ What areas of your life do you believe you need to reflect on?

♥ What motivation(s) do you need to get in prepare mode?

Scriptures

♥ For a week, read and meditate on the scriptures below. Reflect on the message in each scripture and how you can apply it to your daily life during this recovery period.

♥ Day one: Matthew 6:13

♥ Day two: Matthew 4:1-11

♥ Day three: Mark 14:32-38

♥ Day four: Isaiah 26:3

♥ Day five: Psalm 37:23

♥ Day six: Jeremiah 29:11

♥ Day seven: Psalm 30:5

5

DEVIL, DIVA, DAMSEL AND DRAMA QUEEN

During one session, my client decided to bring her best friend for support. I didn't think this was a great idea, but I went along with it because it was an opportunity to see clearly into her world based on the character of the people she surrounded herself with. Her friend, whom I will call Maggie, had a lot to say about my client. Maggie shared with me her opinions regarding what my client should do and why my client was having so many relationship issues. I was impressed by Maggie's insight but I questioned her knowledge and wisdom. I discerned that Maggie's insight came from being hurt by a lot of men and that she had given herself to a lot of men. To prove my point, I provided Maggie with a clean, crisp white sheet of paper and instructed her to write the names of each man she had willingly been sexually involved with. She hesitated and appeared angry at my request but I assured her that my intent was not to disrespect or hurt her but to help my client. After she was done with her list, she handed me the paper and there were 51 names. She had a serious relationship with seven of them. Surprisingly, Maggie had released her power at the age of 13. She recalled each experience as if it had occurred just yesterday. She stated that sex was the only way she knew how to get attention and at a young age she believed it would seal the deal and keep the young man with her. As a young girl, she never understood the value and virtue of her throne.

Each time she would submit her body she submitted her spirit, power and her soul and afterwards she would feel empty, used and unappreciated. Even as an adult, Maggie continued to open her heart to attacks by way of her body. Symbolically, she wanted to be loved, affirmed, valued and protected. She wanted to be "the one" for "him" whoever he was. Unfortunately, Maggie stated she had done some things she was not proud of; asserting at times she didn't recognize or like the woman she had become. She became everything she did not want to be in a relationship- a diva, devil, damsel and drama queen.

Here let's examine the various characteristics that Maggie and other women adapt out of fear when there is a problem in the relationship, separation or break-up.

Damsel- We have heard the saying "damsel in distress." Usually we think about the fairy tales where the princess is in danger and the prince comes along to save her. In a relationship, a hurt woman may become needy and co-dependent looking to the man to take care of her physical and emotional needs. She may communicate that she needs the man to fix something that is broken in her home or car. The woman's motive is to get the man's attention hoping that he will come and see about her. Drastic measures would be lying about medical issues such as being pregnant or severely sick. Being in a relationship with a damsel can be emotionally draining on a man as he may feel smothered and tied down. However, when a damsel is emotionally tired, she may surrender and become a door mat and allow the man to come and go which means the hurt continues.

Diva- The diva appears strong as if she has it all together. She may send the message that she doesn't need the man and is fine all by herself. She can be confusing with her words and actions. The diva woman may say "leave" but her actions may say "stay." The diva will also point out how her world won't fall apart just because the man is not in her life; however she will wait by the phone for him to call, check her emails hoping to have a message, drive by his house to see who is there with him or allow just one last late night rendezvous. Lastly, the diva will assert that she will not take the man back, but each time she does.

Drama Queen- Lights, camera, action! The woman who is a drama queen is fueled by chaos. She pulls the man close as he is trying to leave and then pushes him away as if she doesn't need him. She thrives off the arguments and makes a scene in front of many people. She triangulates the man by including other people in the drama such as his friends, family and his job. The drama queen may cry one minute and is angry the next. She demonstrates a roller coaster of emotions that, in her mind, the man is responsible for.

Devil- The devil is a devious and spiteful woman. She fights back dirty because she is hurt. She scratches the man's car with her keychain, burns or bleaches his clothes, leaves mean messages on his voice mail and verbally attacks him to camouflage her vulnerabilities. The devil woman may experience several anger episodes followed by her developing a plan to hurt the man (revenge). She can be dangerous if her anger is not controlled.

The four characteristics above have something in common which is hurt, pain and heartbreak. In addition, the damsel, diva, devil and drama queen express themselves and seek attention from the man in negative ways. Maggie slashed tires when she became angry with a lover. She lied about being pregnant to keep a man or to get his attention only to "miscarry" the baby later. In addition, Maggie also bleached her ex-boyfriend's clothes and called the police on another lover but refused to press charges. She was fueled by the drama. Even though it was negative attention, it was still attention.

Maggie's presence in that counseling session was powerful and priceless because she helped my client to symbolically see herself in Maggie. Maggie and my client spoke the same language and shared the same heart beat on a symbolic level. Maggie was in no position to provide advice because she had not reclaimed her power, nor had she released the pain and renewed her mind. She continued to think the same irrational way and respond in an emotionally negative manner. Maggie was a hurt woman giving another hurt woman advice.

When a woman is hurt badly, you never know how she may react and you do not know what she may do just to hold on to her man. Compromising yourself for the sake of a man who does not treat you right or make you happy decreases your self-worth. Whatever you have done to keep him, it is okay. No one is here to judge you. The choice you have to make is to stop losing yourself in the relationship. Stop losing your identity so that you will not become a woman you do not recognize or like.

Heart Notes

♥ At this time, focus on your past behaviors, not the man's. What negative behaviors have you shown to receive attention?

♥ What have you done to make a man love you?

♥ What have you done or said in order to keep a man? Did it work?

♥ What negative behaviors do you need to stop immediately?

♥ What did your heart (not your thoughts) want to communicate to the man instead of exhibiting the negative behaviors?

Scriptures

Your adornment must not be merely external- braiding of the hair, and wearing gold jewelry, or putting on dresses; but let it be the hidden person of the heart, with the imperishable quality of a gentle and quiet spirit, which is precious in the sight of God. 1 Peter 3:3-4

A worthless person, a wicked man, is the one who walks with a perverse mouth, who winks with his eyes, who signals with his feet, who points with his fingers; who with perversity in his heart continually devises evil, who spreads strife. Therefore his calamity will come suddenly; instantly he will be broken and there will be no healing. Proverbs 6:12-15

Keeping away from strife is an honor for a man, but any fool will quarrel. Proverbs 20:3

It is better to live in a corner of the roof than in a house shared with a contentious woman. Proverbs 25:24

6
MIND GAMES

The game of chess, in my opinion, challenges your mind. An experienced chess player has spent a lot of time learning the game and the relationship between the chess pieces. Before a move is made it is calculated, analyzed, or investigated. A mature chess player has mastered the process of calculation and analysis, whereby the final decision to move a piece originates from faith. There is no second guessing. An inexperienced chess player may analyze and investigate all of the potential moves which can be overwhelmingly mentally exhausting and mistakes can be made. For that reason, playing chess requires a strategically organized thought process in order to win. Chess is not an emotionally reactive game. When an experienced chess player becomes stumped or frustrated with the game, he does not allow the emotion to decide for him. Instead, the decision is based off of calculation and analysis. Why am I sharing this information with you? Because it is time for you to stop allowing men to play these mind games with you. It is time for you to reclaim your power by recognizing who you are. In chess, the most powerful chess piece is the queen because she can be moved in any direction.

You are the queen, the most powerful game piece, and you have the control to move in any direction you choose simply by exerting the power of positive thinking. Whenever you have a decision to make you have fear or faith as your two choices. Fear is best friends with a lot of women. Fear moves into a woman's heart, mind and home. It settles into a woman's day-to-day life ushering her to make decisions with it in mind. Fear tells a woman to stay when she should go. Fear keeps a woman from success, passion and love. Fear communicates with revenge, anger, depression and insecurity. Fear holds a board meeting to discuss which emotion will take over a woman's heart and fear sets the bylaws for how to keep a woman in a relationship with it. Fear does not ever want to be alone because fear has no confidence; fear does not trust.

Faith, on the other hand, is the opposite of fear. Faith hangs out with assertiveness, hope, confidence, honesty, transparency and freedom. Faith embraces a woman and supports her to be her best self. Faith is a wonderful ally to have if you can handle all of faith's awesomeness; it embodies royalty and it leads you to success in life. You don't have to worry about if faith will fit you or not because it's a one size fits all kind of deal. Believe it or not, you already have a faith muscle you just need to flex it so that it can get bigger and stronger.

The majority of the time, a hurt woman who is not ready to let go of an unhealthy relationship responds out of fear. Do you have any idea what your fear-driven decisions look like? Think about the job you didn't apply for because you thought you weren't good enough. Or what about the decision you made to stay in the relationship because you didn't want to lose the material things that he provided? Do you remember the time you stayed in an unhealthy relationship because you didn't want to start all over again with someone else? Or what about the time you felt so good about yourself but once you arrived to the party and saw other beautiful women you stepped into your shadow and sat in a corner? These are all decisions made out of fear.

A decision from faith, on the other hand, requires confidence, assertiveness, and hope. Need I say it again? Your Higher Power will give you the same lesson over and over until you master it. The lesson here is to honor yourself; all of you. In the past, you made your decision out of fear. Now it is time to exercise your faith to see different results. It all boils down to how you think, what you feel and how you react.

For example, whenever someone attends a therapy session I have to decide what treatment modality to use to "treat" the client's issue. There are many options; however the most common treatment model is Cognitive Behavioral Therapy (CBT). The first premise of CBT is your thoughts affect how you will feel which means what you think about a situation that happens to you will affect how you will feel. Say for instance a man lies to you and you say, "He hurt me" when in fact according to the theory of CBT, your negative thoughts caused you to hurt more; not the man's actions.

This can be hard for some women to accept so let's look at this closer so that you may understand.

Life happens and will always happen, which also means situations happen. Do you agree so far? Okay, say for instance you find out the man lied to you and he was cheating. That's the situation or in CBT it is called the event or trigger.

Once you found out the man lied, you began to think, "He ain't no good," "He is a liar," "He doesn't love me." These are negative thoughts, right? Of course these are negative thoughts. According to the CBT theory, we have two types of thinking patterns- negative and positive. Once again, your negative thoughts are magnifying the cheating situation and as a result you begin to feel more hurt, sad or angry. You might think about who he cheated with, what she looked like, what they did together and where. Its thoughts like these that make you feel worse; not the man. Agree so far? Well, probably at this point you are saying, "I don't know about this CBT stuff; he cheated on me." Once again, a statement like that is a fact but do not give the action of cheating or the man power of you.

The second concept of CBT asserts your thoughts affect how you feel. So now you are thinking negative thoughts about being cheated on without the man having to say or do anything. Right now, this is all occurring inside your head at the speed of light. As a result of thinking, "He's a liar," "He is no good," you continue to feel sad, depressed, worthless, hurt or angry.

After the trigger (hearing your man has cheated), negative thoughts ("He is a liar", "He doesn't love me.") and the feelings (sad, angry, etc.) then the behavior happens. So what type of behaviors are you likely to show? You may respond by crying, arguing, looking for answers, over-eating, or you may sleep less or more. It depends but this list can go on and on. Lastly, there is a consequence for your behavior. As a result of over-eating you may gain weight or due to the arguing with your man the relationship will be tense, disconnected and it could end. You probably think CBT is depressing by now, but it is not.

Here is where I add two important aspects, fear or faith, to the CBT model. Basically, you cannot control or change the man and you cannot control or change what the man has done, but you can control how you respond to the situation. It is normal for you to have negative or self-defeating thoughts, but those negative thoughts can be changed by you. Once again, you are the Queen and you have the power to change how you will feel and respond to the negative situation. Let's look at this same situation again and reframe the negative thoughts.

One, the man cheats which is basically an emotional violation. Next, identify what emotional boundary he violated. Third, you think he is no good and so forth. Now, it is okay to think whatever you want to think but the goal is for you not to magnify the situation with your negative thoughts. Okay so at that moment, interject the fear or faith model. You can stay on the road of negative thoughts that will spiral you out of control (fear) or you can exercise your faith muscle.

Reclaim your power and begin to release some of that pain by reframing the negative thought. For example, you could say, "This dude did the ultimate no, no. This is an emotional violation of my emotional boundaries and I will not accept it." Okay, that was kind of long and you might not say it like that, but you get the point. Do not compromise yourself and do not give energy to who the other woman is and what he does with her. With faith, you instantly give power to yourself and not the situation or man. You choose not to engage in a power struggle with him to get answers, attention or commitment.

Faith says you will be okay. Faith also says you deserve better and your worth is priceless. As a result, you may begin to feel empowered because you know you deserve better. Of course the action of cheating will hurt, but your declaration of self-worth and honoring your emotional boundaries will strengthen you. The behaviors you might exhibit at that time could be walking away from the relationship and the consequence could be you will be hurt less and feel more empowered later on. Agree so far? Like I said, it is so hard for people to understand how their negative thoughts magnify a situation or how they feel about an incident. There is a chart below for you to practice this model until you can honor it. Once you understand how you are in control of the intensity of your pain, you will know how to minimize your heart attacks and maximize your self-worth. Remember, we get the same lesson over and over until we master it.

I have another scenario for you. A woman had been in a relationship with her man for 10 years and desperately wanted to be married. This guy had asked her to marry him several times but only when he had screwed up and hurt her tremendously. This was his weapon; he knew which card to play to get her back and he won every time. Well here she was years later and still no marriage; same guy, same drama. I am always shocked whenever she is hurt regarding him cheating. I mean, that's what he does. He has consistently demonstrated he is a liar, cheater and a disrespectful man. I had her to revisit her emotional boundaries list and she identified cheating as the emotional violation. Her thoughts were, "I can't believe he did this to me again." I responded, "Yes, you can and you should believe it because he never showed you anything different." She went on to say, "I have put in so much time in this relationship that I can't get back." My response was, "Each time he cheated and each time he proposed you decided to stay. He did not make you stay so you pimped yourself and you wasted your time. You made your decision out of fear."

Next, I pushed her to exercise her faith muscle just this one time regarding this man. I told her to take a deep breath and let all the fear come into her mind and give it time to flow out. I asked her to keep breathing and then tell me what she wanted. She said, "I just want to be loved. I don't want anyone to hurt me anymore." I asked her did she want it bad enough and she said she did. This woman had the power to stop this man from hurting her. All she had to do was make a decision. I instructed her to use faith to make her decision; either choose herself or him. At the end of her session I told her not to come back until she had made the choice out of faith. That, my friend, was her spiritual challenge or lesson to learn. It was a test to measure her strength and self-love. This man was only the vessel being used to teach her this lesson. Simply put, she had to put on the whole armor of self-love. Do you remember that from chapter four? Well, in the end she made a decision but it took her almost a year to choose herself and to choose faith.

I do not want you to be like her; I don't want another year to go by for you with more heart attacks. Heck, I don't want another year to go by and you are still in the same lousy relationship wasting your life away. At this point you may have been doing a lot of thinking and a lot of feeling. Consequently, it is very easy for some people to offer advice to you regarding your relationships by saying, "If I were you, I would do..." The problem is they are not you and they probably could not handle walking in your shoes. Be very careful about listening to "if I were you advice." It is not always a wise thing to listen to what other women would do if they were you because this is emotionally reactive advice. I caution you on quickly reacting emotionally because a wise woman thinks before speaking and a foolish woman has loose lips. According to the scripture, you must be quick to hear, slow to speak and slow to anger (James 1:19). It requires self-control and a certain level of wisdom. Knowledge comes from understanding and wisdom is your ability to apply that knowledge each day. The primary reason I included the CBT model in this book is because I want you to understand how powerful your thoughts are and how thinking negatively can affect your relationships and your life. You can learn from your mistakes and apply that knowledge in every aspect of your life. Remember your Higher Power will give you the same lesson over and over until you master it. You master the current lesson by looking at the previous lessons you failed and correcting your responses. Nothing comes easy as it requires practice every moment of your life.

Use the chart below to practice changing your thoughts.

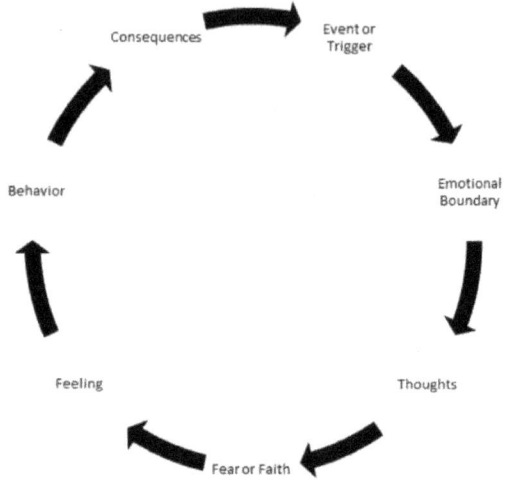

Consequences

Event or Trigger

Emotional Boundary

Behavior

Thoughts

Feeling

Fear or Faith

Heart Notes

♥ What are the negative thoughts you have had related to previous break-ups?
♥ What will be the most difficult part for you, changing your thoughts or choosing faith?

Scriptures

...be transformed by the renewing of your mind... Romans 12.2

And He said to them, "Why are you afraid? Do you still have no faith?" Mark 4:40

Like a city that is broken into and without walls is a man who has no control over his spirit. Proverbs 25:28

7
THUGS, PIMPS AND PLAYAS

A few years ago, my favorite person treated me to a manicure and pedicure; however it was not at my usual spot. Instead, we stopped at a nail salon in the West End, a neighborhood located in Atlanta. While my feet were soaking, I listened to four women talk about their relationship problems. Some of it was hilarious, but a lot of it was terrible. Interestingly enough, if I would have closed my eyes, I swear it would have sounded like the same woman talking. Think about the language hurt women use to describe men. All men are _____. If you lay down with _____ you will get up with fleas. Men are __-down, dirty _____. He's a _____ and a _____. Women communicate their painful experiences by describing men using negative connotations. It's a form of wounded talk that is not empowering and it keeps you feeling hurt and when another woman speaks the same language you may feel some sort of a connection.

It is an overgeneralization to say all men are dogs. It is like saying all women are gold diggers, which is not true. Whenever people use the term, gold digger, to refer to a woman it is usually used in a negative way to insinuate the woman only wants money or materialistic things. In addition, the urban dictionary goes on to negatively capitalize on the gold digging term depicting it as a sexual act. Gold is a precious and valuable metal and is highly sought after. It lies at the core of the earth and has to be accessed by way of mining or digging. It is a calculated and rigorous process which requires skill and patience. Ironically, I encourage you to be a gold digger in a positive context, in that I want you to dig deep to get to know a man. Get to know his character and the core of his heart because it will determine his value. Focus on what is truly important to you when you are digging deep for the gold. It is important for you to assess the type of men you have been attracting in your life. Remember, you will receive the same lesson over and over until you master. The only difference is it has been the same message, same guy with a different face.

Luckily, I have categorized men who draw women's power away from them into three categories: thugs, pimps and playas. In my opinion, there is nothing about these titles that says faithful, respectful and honorable. Does this mean that thugs, pimps and playas are not good men? No, this is not what I am saying. I am sure there are some thugs, pimps and playas with good hearts; however it's their lifestyle that may be questionable. What I am saying is it is not wise to get involved with a thug's lifestyle if you are trying to stay away from heart attacks. If you want a long-term commitment, it is not wise for you to roll with a pimp or a playa knowing what he is involved in and who he is involved with. Whenever you find yourself wishing certain character traits were different about a man or wanting to change him, then it means wrong man at the wrong time. What's important is the character of the man and his values.

Sometimes women develop a list of characteristics such as handsome, great body, great sex, good job, car, his own house, Christian and no kids. A list like this says nothing about a man's character. Think about the checklist you have used in the past and how easy it was for a thug, pimp or playa to meet your approval. The issue always begins with the heart and character of a man.

Thugs, pimps and playas know exactly what women are looking for and they do not present themselves as a wolf in sheep's clothing. Nine times out of ten, a thug, pimp and playa show you exactly who they are except you do not believe them. Why? Because it felt good to have "some" of your needs met. It felt good to have his attention or affection; bottom line is he made you feel good. They are well capable of wooing a woman and meeting her needs temporarily. Ultimately it is not about you and your needs it's about him and what he can get from you and many more women.

Men are smart creatures, but not smart enough to really figure a woman out. Why do you think women are a mystery to men at times? Heck, Adam did not witness Eve being created because he was asleep. Even though men may say they do not understand women, they understand how to use, manipulate and identify a woman's challenge or weak areas. Men are aware when they are in a relationship with an insecure woman. Men are also aware when they are dealing with a woman who does not respect herself because they know their games do not fly with a woman who respects herself. Men also do not play games when they respect a woman. They know when they have a strong-willed, intelligent, loving, free, secure and faith-driven woman. Men also know a wounded, crazy, broken, desperate and insecure woman when he sees her. Men only know these things about women because women have played the game of chess on the man's chess board without knowing the power of being the queen piece. When you reclaim your power, release the pain and stop participating in a man's game, he will not understand your heart and mind because you will be speaking a different language and operating on different rules. Haven't you heard a man admit that it can be difficult to figure a woman out? It is because a man is comfortable playing by his rules, but a touch down or slam dunk won't happen if he doesn't have home court advantage. Once you change the rules on them, they are required to hustle.

The best hustlers are thugs, pimps and playas. A thug hustles in the street, a pimp hustles for money and a playa hustles women. A thug is a man who is a connoisseur of the streets; he has street smarts. The thug may have a criminal record or he may not. He may carry a gun and even if he doesn't carry a gun he knows where to get one. The thug is also creative with his career; he may be self-employed, unemployed, or employed.

A pimp is the Chief Executive Officer of disrespecting women because he doesn't give a damn. He gets what he wants by any means necessary. The pimp will use a woman to make money or have her give him money. A woman may be asked to buy a pair of sneakers, provide gas money, groceries, or sell her body. Pimps openly admit to having a lot of women at their disposal sexually.

On the contrary, a playa thinks he is so smooth and he is. The playa has smooth words, smooth kisses and smooth touches. He is smooth because he knows what to say to a woman and when to say it. He is able to get a lot of women because he connects to their needs in order to have his needs met. Understand I did not say a playa meets a woman's needs. He is aware of what she needs and lets her know that he recognizes her needs but he does not always meet all of her needs. He makes the woman feel as though she is the one and he makes the other women feel the same as well.

Now the terms playa and pimp can be used synonymously in the streets. Often times, men may be called a pimp because they have a lot of women. In the streets, a playa or pimp is like a badge of honor. I have seen white collar pimps and playas who are well-educated and employed. A white-collar pimp or playa has a lot of money; however a woman will have to earn it. A successful male client shared with me how he wined and dined a young woman for a few months because he wanted to sleep with her. Apparently she played hard-to-get in the beginning but all of the wining and dining spoiled her and it was a touchdown for him.

Falling in love with an active-duty thug, pimp or playa is not advised. It spells heart attack. No matter if the man is blue collar, white collar, thug, pimp, playa, doctor, lawyer or preacher it is the character and values of a man that truly count. Now don't get me wrong; thugs, pimps and playas can be redeemed which means they can change. They can grow up, mature and become new men or shall I say new creatures. And when a good man decides to love you, it will not be painful because love does not hurt. Even though a lot of people loosely say, "love hurts" it is not true. Love does not hurt; the people we love or who say they love us are the ones who hurt us but the act of love is not painful at all.

I had to educate a young woman on the meaning of love as she had it all twisted. Her boyfriend told her that she was his "main girl." She wore the title like a badge of honor. Unfortunately, she did not like the way she felt whenever he did not treat her like the main girl. You see, her boyfriend made it perfectly clear that he had other women; he had a V.I.P. list and her name was at the top. I shared with her that he had the power to change the list whenever he pleased by deleting or adding a woman. Love is kind which means the man is kind and respectful. Love is patient and never rude or condescending. Love is supportive, giving and uplifting; it is not jealous or arrogant. Love is not selfish and it is not wishy-washy. Love is consistent and it never fails or fade. Love feels good. A man that loves you is mindful of you and he will not nor will he have the intention of deceiving or hurting you. There is nothing confusing or imbalanced about love.

Character and Values

In chapter six, I provided the chess game analogy to explain how powerful the position of a Queen is. In chess, the most important piece is the King. Isn't it interesting that the queen is the most powerful piece and the king is the most important? The reason the king is important is because the objective of the game is to "checkmate" or capture the king. Ironically, this makes the king the weakest piece as well because the king's goal is not to be captured. You may ask, "Why is she sharing more chess rules with me?" The reason is because you are a queen and deep in your heart you want a king, but you must understand the process of capturing him.

The millionaire matchmaker, Patti Stanger, has a rule when she introduces her client to his or her potential date. The rule is, "no sex before monogamy." Sometimes the client has a difficult time following this rule; more so the male client than the female. I think it is a great rule to have, so etch it in your heart because emotional intimacy should come before physical intimacy. Do you remember the young girl, Maggie, earlier in the book? She had 51 sex partners and not one successful relationship. Maggie dated a lot of thugs, pimps and playas. Quite honestly, that's what Maggie was attracted to. She focused on the outside because she was emotionally immature. Focusing on emotional intimacy requires you to dig for the gold which will help you to assess a man's emotional maturity. Yes, that is right, his emotional maturity will let you know if he is a teenage boy hibernating in a grown man's body. If so, run like hell.

First let me explain what I mean by emotional immaturity. Emotional immaturity is the man who needs to be the center of attention; he needs to have his ego stroked. A man who is insecure is also emotionally immature. In addition, the emotionally immature man feels he needs to "get back at you" and he operates with the spirit of the seven deadly sins. What do I mean by this? A man who is greedy, full of pride, lazy, lustful, envious, angry and full of gluttony is emotionally immature because these sins are full of selfishness. Also add the stalkers, abusers, and chauvinists to the list. Quite frankly, any man who cannot express his emotions openly, honestly, and respectfully is emotionally immature.

Three years ago I received a phone call from a man wanting to schedule an appointment with me. He wanted to come in as soon as possible so I saw him the very next day. He was a well-dressed, sweet-smelling, tall, handsomely groomed man. The brother was hot, but not that kind of hot. He was a hot mess. Basically, he was a playa whose game was slipping. He had women problems. Each week, I sat for an hour and listened to him go on and on about how this woman was finding out about that woman. His game was slipping and I wanted to know why. I asked him did he really come to counseling to talk about how he was getting caught with other women or was it something else? He honestly admitted that he was tired of the game and he wanted more from a woman; however the women he was fooling around with weren't good enough. In other words, they were missing that "je ne sais quoi" which was something that he needed but could not describe. Anyway, he told me about an old lover that he wanted back in his life except she would not give him a chance. She had moved on with her life because she was tired of him playing games. He said that she wouldn't touch him with a ten foot pole. She sounded like a smart woman to me, but I could see that he really cared about her and wanted to be with her except he didn't know where to start. I knew at that moment that those three weeks of just listening to him had paid off because he was ready for emotional maturation. This brother was ready to make the changes within his character and values to have the woman he wanted.

Character will reveal who a man is within the core of his heart. Values are important in a man because values communicate what is truly important to him. His values may be God, family and future or drugs, sex and money. Even if he talks a good game, his actions will communicate his values. What values are important to you? The man you are interested in must have values congruent to yours. If you value prayer and he does not believe in God then that is an issue. What type of character is important to you? If being dependable is a characteristic that you feel strongly about in a partner then a man who is undependable and wishy-washy is not for you. You are not God; you cannot change anyone. You can be an influencer but not a changer. Only the man can make the choice to change which means he, too, has a decision to make.

Now a lot of folks say opposites attract and that may be true. In life, opposites are all around us- good and bad, black and white, up and down, truth or lie. However, if you and a man are completely opposite until where it causes problems in the relationship, then don't force it. When considering characteristics and values focus on the positive ones and be cognizant of the negatives. Do not ignore the warning signs because your Higher Power will give you the same lesson over and over until you master it. Do not be like Maggie and keep picking the same guys; you have to go gold digging.

Any warning signs you see in a man, consider them as your study notes. Your study notes will help you master the test and avoid a few heart attacks. You have to know what you want in a man. When a man decides to settle down and get serious with a woman, he knows exactly what he is looking for. Right now, identify the characteristics that are important to you in a partner. The list below is a short-list to help you get started.

Use your journal to develop your character and values checklist.

Trustworthy	Dishonest
Loving	Liar
Kind	Unfaithful
Responsible	Irresponsible
Faithful	Undependable
Supportive	Selfish
Respectful	Disrespectful
Patient	Lazy
Dependable	Unstable
Committed	Deceitful
Ethical	Conceit
Spiritual	Greed

Heart Notes

♥ What do you value? Do you think it is wise to be in a relationship with a man with different values than yours?

♥ What red flags did you ignore that were revealed in a man?

♥ What difficult lesson did you learn from the relationship(s)?

♥ If you would have adhered to the red flags, what would the lesson have been?

Scriptures

Therefore if anyone is in Christ, he is a new creature; the old things passed away; behold, new things have come. 2 Corinthians 5:17

Wait for the Lord; be strong and let your heart take courage; yes, wait for the Lord. Psalm 27:14

Do not be unequally yoked with unbelievers. For what partnership has righteousness with lawlessness? Or what fellowship has light with darkness? 2 Corinthians 6:14

But the Lord said to Samuel, do not look at his appearance or at the height of his stature, because I have rejected him; for God sees not as man sees, for man looks at the outward appearance, but the Lord looks at the heart. 1 Samuel 16:7

RENEW AND PREPARE

8
COMMUNICATING FROM YOUR HEART

Humans are born to communicate. Even at birth babies begin to communicate their needs and wants in their own special way by crying. Little children also have several ways of communicating their allegiance or commitment to one another. They may swear on the bible, pinky promise or cross their heart. These gestures symbolize being truthful and loyal. Adults do not depend on pinky promises and bible swearing; instead we depend on the other person to be honest. Unfortunately, sometimes life teaches adults to put away the loyalty and truth of a child due to painful experiences. This causes us to be on guard as a means of protection.

Nevertheless, you must admit that effective interpersonal communication skills is not taught in school. Communication is something you learn as you continue to live longer. You either get better at it or you don't. A lot of people learn their communication style from their family. Did you witness a family member raise their voice or scream to get others to listen? Did someone give the silent treatment whenever they were angry? Or did you experience an open, loving way of communicating? Communication styles are modeled in families every day, some are effective and some are ineffective. We take what we learn from our families and as we grow, our communication style may change. The best communication is honest, pure, nonjudgmental and respectful. Fear keeps you from communicating in this manner. Once you face the fear and honor yourself with truthfulness, you can communicate from your heart.

Communicating from your heart requires honesty, transparency and vulnerability. Vulnerability does not mean weakness, in this sense, it means to communicate without fear; it is the strength and courage to communicate the truth. You let go of the fear of the other person being upset with you, the fear of not pleasing someone, the fear of hurting the person's feelings or the fear of an argument starting.

The basic communication tips to remember are: communicate, compromise and connect. As the communicator you should:

♥ Use "I" messages to explain how you feel. For example, "When you ignore me I feel hurt."

♥ Be specific about what you want and need such as, "I need you to be patient with me and take the time to listen without rushing me." "I want you to put aside your distractions and focus on us for fifteen minutes."

♥ Ask your partner if he is able to meet your need? If not, then begin to communicate a compromise.

♥ Listen to each other. If you are thinking about what you want to say while your partner is talking then you are not listening, you are preparing your rebuttal.

♥ Exercise patience and respect during the conversation. If what you have to say cannot be communicated in a respectful tone, then take a time out and come back later. It takes two to argue.

♥ Recognize what your hot buttons are. We all have them. What normally ticks you off and fuels an argument?

I have a rule of thumb to always handle the other person's spirit as gently as possible. In other words, if what you have to say cannot be communicated in a respectful and loving manner, then do not say anything at all. Period. Always deposit something positive into the relationship because you cannot take back negative things or hurtful words. Lastly, if all else fails use the toss, tag and tease method. If the topic is petty, then toss it; do not exert your energy on it. If the topic has the potential of getting heated and may turn into an argument, then tag it for later. Use the tag as a form of time-out for yourself and your partner. Think about what you want to say and use the techniques above to help you sort through how you will communicate it. Next, if the topic is important to you and you want to talk more about it, then tease it. Only tease the topic, or go deeper, if your partner is open, calm and engages the tease with a respectful response. Also, my favorite question to connect with someone is, "What's been on your heart and mind lately?" The person usually opens up versus saying, "Nothing." If you ask someone, "How do you feel?" they just may say, "Fine" even if it is not true. Just make sure you reframe your questions to get the person to go deeper.

I understand that changing how you communicate can be difficult, especially if it does not feel natural to you. For the most part, people are used to flying off the handle or should I say getting someone told. Have you ever gone off and given a man a piece of your mind? Was it effective? Probably 80% of the time it is not effective because most men become turtles and either shut down verbally by not talking, shut down emotionally by not opening up, or shut down physically by leaving. To decrease going off on someone, let's also review the difference between excuses, arguments and secrecy.

Excuse versus Explanation

There is a difference between an excuse and an explanation. When a man is dishonest, you do not want to hear his excuse or whatever lie he has concocted because he will only be thinking about himself and what he may lose or gain. An excuse is an act of selfishness. An explanation, on the other hand, is an act of accountability. Instead, you want to hear him explain his actions and be accountable. The man who is accountable for his actions will provide the truth. Even if he is fearful of what he may lose; he will present the truth. It is difficult for women who have had multiple heart attacks to receive the truth at times because it may hurt them more or it is not what they want to hear. A man that says, "It's not you it's me" is giving an excuse.

There was a couple I provided counseling to some years ago. They were not married; just dating and living together. The woman was upset that her boyfriend stayed out late, drinking, playing cards, etc. During each session she would look at him and ask, "Why won't you come home at night and who are you with?" Each time, he provided a different excuse. They were good answers but I could tell he wasn't giving her the truth. One excuse was he was too drunk to drive home. Another time he stated he didn't want to come in and wake her and the kids. In my opinion, this dude was full of excuses. The next session they attended, I decided to help this sister out and I told her to remove the 'why' questions from her vocabulary. I instructed her to replace the 'why' with 'tell me the reason.' I also instructed him to let go of any fears he had about giving her the truth and explain to her what was going on. This time she looked at him and said, "Tell me the reason you don't come home at night." He sat quietly staring at me with a slight smirk on his face as if he was thinking, "Is she for real?" I gestured to him to answer the question. He looked her dead in the eyes and said, "Because I don't want to hear your mouth." I was shocked and so was she. He went on to share how he would rather stay away than to deal with her "yapping and complaining." He did not like to argue and after hanging out and having fun he knew he couldn't go home in peace because, according to him, she would ruin it. The point here is not about what this man was doing when he was out of the house. The point is recognizing the difference between an excuse and an explanation and how to get an explanation out of someone. If the man has made up his mind to lie, he will lie. Men lie for so many reasons such as fear of hurting the woman, fear of getting in trouble, fear of being caught, judged, or wanting to be right.

Disagreements versus Arguments

A disagreement is when two people do not share the same ideas and opinions. No one is wrong in a disagreement just respect and honor the other's opinions and move on. Remember, you cannot change anyone. Arguments, however, involve criticism, judgment and disrespect. The goal of an argument is to win, be heard, and get your point across. When a man says, "Okay, so you're right and I'm wrong," or "That's how it is-you're right" he is not agreeing with you he is being sarcastic and disrespectful. It's still an argument. Effective communication cannot occur during an argument because no one is listening and no one is open. During a disagreement, it may be possible to be heard and have a meaningful conversation to resolve the issue only if both parties are listening. Write this down…if you are thinking about what you want to say while the other person is talking then you are not listening. Listening requires your undivided attention. If you are truly listening, then whatever the person is saying will matter to you. It's a symbol of respect. I didn't say what the person is saying is right. I am saying their thoughts and feelings should matter to you, especially if you love them. Now, if for some reason you are in a relationship and the man does not listen and honor your thoughts and feelings then it should be a done deal. Period. I'm sure an emotional boundary has been violated at that time it's just up to you to honor it.

Privacy versus Secrecy

There is a distinct difference between privacy and secrecy. Many times in a relationship women do not have a clear understanding of the two and as a result are not able to set realistic emotional boundaries. Private matters, when revealed in a relationship, will not hurt you or your partner. Things that are private may consist of your goals in life, how often you get paid at work, things you daydream about, your credit score or how much money you have in your bank account. Secrecy, on the other hand, is intentional and when revealed will hurt you or your partner emotionally. Secrecy could involve dating someone else while in a committed relationship, lying about your whereabouts or who you are spending time with, connecting with an ex on Facebook, flirting or physical intimacy with another person.

I have a good example for you. A married lady came to see me because she wanted couples counseling. She came alone because she wanted to see if I would keep her secret. She disclosed having an affair with a co-worker. In addition, she also discovered her husband was having an affair after going through his cell phone and email account. She was upset with his betrayal. As a result, she did some detective work and found out where the mistress lived, went to her house, and proceeded to put the beat down on her in front of the woman's husband. The married lady then shared with me that she would not be divorcing her husband because he is sorry for what he did, blah, blah, blah and she did not want to lose her home, nice car, and vacations. Even though her husband was not aware of her affair, she decided she was not going to end the affair with her co-worker. She asked me to never mention her secret to her husband. My answer was, "Hell no." I told her that I do not start a relationship with my clients with secrets. I would not allow her to pimp me like that or have power over me in such a way. It is different if I am counseling someone and later down the road they disclose a secret. I can definitely keep a secret because I know at some point the therapy will help them open up about it, but I was not about to start a therapeutic relationship built on secrecy and lies because it violates the four principles of a healthy relationship- trust, support, patience and respect. Long story short, I never saw the married lady again after that because she didn't like what I had to say. There are people who believe "what someone doesn't know won't hurt them." I guess that may be true but I believe there are some truths that won't go to the grave with us. Secrets are like cancers of the heart; it will eat at your conscience every day and sooner or later the truth will come out. You do not have to force it.

Heart Notes
- ♥ What did your family teach you about communication?
- ♥ What are your hot buttons that trigger an argument?
- ♥ What are your fears about being transparent when you communicate?
- ♥ How do you know when a man is listening to you?
- ♥ Which communication technique will you implement?

Scriptures

A gentle answer turns away wrath, but a harsh word stirs up anger. Proverb 15:1

Pleasant words are a honeycomb, sweet to the soul and healing to the bones. Proverbs 16:24

He who restrains his words has knowledge, and he who has a cool spirit is a man of understanding. Proverbs 17:27

Would not God find this out? For He knows the secrets of the heart. Psalm 44:21

9
THE 'F' WORD

It's not what you think so get your head out of the gutter. In fact, the 'F' word I am talking about is forgiveness. My mission here is not about getting you to forgive whomever has hurt you. Forgiving others is a noble thing to do, in fact the bible instructs us to forgive. However in this case, the forgiveness is for you. Whenever you hold on to the painful memories, hurt, disappointments and every detail of each betrayal, you also hold yourself hostage. Being held hostage does not allow you the freedom to be happy. Forgiveness, in this sense, is choosing to free yourself. That is the first step. Once again you are back to square one with making a choice. You, him or them? Making a decision to forgive means you are making a decision to live your best life without emotional restraints. Forgiveness equals freedom and freedom equals happiness. Nelson Mandela taught the world the art of forgiveness. He had every right not to forgive, yet he valued his inner freedom more than any hatred or revenge. You could learn a lot from him.

Many people believe that forgiving the person who hurt them is letting them off the hook or acknowledging that what they did was okay. Be clear that this is not what I am saying. Making a decision to forgive is very difficult because there are many, many memories to sort through and let go of. It is your decision regarding how much of the pain you will hold on to and for how long.

A young lady called me to schedule an appointment. She said she wanted counseling to help with her depression. The following week she came into the office to begin her therapy. She noted the origin of her depression stemmed from a rape that had occurred a few months ago. Apparently, she had been flirting with her accuser for a few weeks and had gone out on two dates with him. Unfortunately, the young man thought her 'no' meant 'yes.' She was upset with herself and felt guilty. She blamed herself for the rape saying, "I shouldn't have flirted with him like that." The fact is, the rape was not her fault. She had no control over that man's thoughts or actions. She needed to forgive herself because her guilt was holding her hostage.

In contrast, a very dear friend of mine was in a relationship with a young man she truly loved. There were good times and bad times but more good than bad. Occasionally, he would tell her that she wasn't the prettiest girl he had dated. At times, he talked down to her and made her question her worth. I can remember her saying, "If only he didn't drink so much or if only he didn't party so late." She was not a clubbing type of girl; she was ready to settle down but struggled with the two of them being so different. On good days, her boyfriend would cook her the best meals and take her to the nicest places. In fact, one nice place was a trip out of the country for her birthday. One summer, she left work early and they headed to the airport flying off to Mexico. It was the worst trip ever! She did not know that trip would be a defining point in her life because she had to make a decision. Her or him?

Unfortunately, he became so drunk he choked her and slammed her head on the taxi cab window during an argument. There she was millions of miles away from home and this dude wanted to get violent. She could see her life flash before her eyes and for the first time she chose not to ignore the warning signs. Once they returned home, he complained about not having any money and how he thought she was going to pay for half of the trip. I can remember thinking, "Damn girl, it was your birthday so how is he going to ask you to pay for a trip that he volunteered to take you on?"

A week later, she made reservations at a nice restaurant. In fact, it was a place he mentioned wanting to dine in. She called him and asked him to meet her at the restaurant for dinner and he did. He ordered, they ate, and then she handed him a white envelope. He opened the envelope and there inside was four hundred dollars. She said,

> "Even though the trip was your idea and your gift to me, I wanted to pay you back. The money is for my half of the hotel room and the cost of food I ate while on the trip. We had buddy passes for the flight so we are even on that. Never do I want to take anything from any man who doesn't want to give it to me with love. So I will take my heart back and you take your four hundred dollars and we go our separate ways."

She walked out of that restaurant with class, power, and all of her self-worth glowing all over her. She was hurt, but not one time was she tempted to call him or see him. She had put on the whole armor of self-love and for the first time she admitted that his character and values were not what she wanted in a man. She forgave herself for wasting time in the relationship and she forgave herself for not standing up to him a long time ago. She admitted she was afraid of being alone because she thought he was as good as it would get for her. It did, however, take her a long time to forgive him for all the mean words and disrespectful things he had said and done to her. She has never forgotten what he said and did and she has never allowed how he hurt her to have power over her life and future. Forgive yourself first.

Friendship

The other 'F' word is friendship which is the first serious relationship for a lot of people. Do you remember your first friend and how the relationship started? I'm sure the friendship started because there was a friendly connection, you had a lot in common, and it was easy to talk about anything. Friendships are a woman's support system; it's where women open up and show who they are. Women reveal their true selves to their girlfriends which can make the bond tighter. In a friendship, a woman is either a good friend or not so good friend. Nevertheless, it is the "not-so-good friends" that women have to decide to keep or let go of. I say this because when you decide to work on yourself and open your heart to personal growth, you may outgrow some people.

Ironically, friendships teach us about fear, faith and forgiveness. In friendships there are lies, betrayal, gossip, judgment, truth, greed, pride, happiness, love, loyalty, failures, success, brokenness, strength, tears, guilt, support and guidance. In friendships, your insecurities are revealed or protected. Unfortunately, women can be hurt by their girlfriends too. In fact, your girlfriend has the potential of hurting you more than a man would because of the vulnerability you might have shown her. Think about it, women know women. We often know their strengths and weaknesses and we also go for the jugular when we decide to attack. There is nothing scarier than a revengeful woman or should I say crazy woman. A woman can be so supportive, loyal and loving. She can be your road dog, therapist, and partner in crime. On the contrary, a friend can be jealous, sneaky, stab you in the back, smile in your face, plot to take your place, and so much more.

Recently, I read a journal entry whereby the young lady wrote about a friend who acted like she was so supportive but deep in her heart the young friend was deceitful, sneaky and jealous. This so-called friend began to defame the young lady's name throughout their circle which ruined so many relationships for her. This young lady was in relationship repair mode. The emotional boundary was betrayal and the emotional violation was gossip. The young lady decided it was best to end their friendship. Had she ignored the emotional violation by the friend, I am positive that there would have been many more painful experiences in their friendship. I believe her ex-friend was a major sabotage; so know that it is okay to put some people off your ship. This young lady was able to accomplish goals in her career and in new relationships after letting go of the friendship. Just like this young lady, you have a choice to make- You or them? You may meet your old friends later on in life but right now you are heading in a different direction.

It is not uncommon for me to ask God to reveal my snakes to me. I do this because I want to be aware of the people who are close to me but mean me no good. Each time, it has been a female friend. Fortunately, I made the decision to let go of a lot of "friends" because their character revealed a part of them that was not what I wanted to associate with. In other words, I did not want them to be a part of my entourage. However, I have forgiven them in my heart so that I could move on with no hatred.

Just like trees in the forest, some grow faster and taller than others. At some point you will look around and notice that some girlfriends haven't grown yet and then there are some friends who have had a growth spurt. Surround yourself with growing women or grown, wise women. Once again, go gold digging to make sure you see the character of your girlfriends' heart. Think about who will be a part of your entourage.

Be sure to choose the "friends with benefits" package. Basically, your girlfriends should have good emotional stocks as well. If they do, they will be more likely to "benefit" you. Girlfriends with diversified emotional stocks support and encourage you. They lift you up and highlight your best self. They see you for who you are and they accept you; however they expect nothing but the best from you because they know your strengths and what you are capable of. As for your girlfriends who have stunted growth because of their heart defects, let go because they too have a choice to make.

Heart Notes

♥ Is there anything you need to forgive yourself for?

♥ Who do you need to forgive so that you can move on?

♥ Do you have any friends you need to let go of for now?

♥ Who are they?

Scriptures

Pride goes before destruction, and a haughty spirit before stumbling. Proverbs 16:18

For if you forgive others for their transgressions, your heavenly Father will forgive you. Matthew 6: 14

...But you are a God of forgiveness, gracious and compassionate, slow to anger and abounding in loving kindness; and you did not forsake them. Nehemiah 9:17

A man of too many friends comes to ruin, but there is a friend who sticks closer than a brother. Proverbs 18:24

10
EMOTIONAL STOCK MARKET

Pay yourself first! In chapter one, you made the choice to choose yourself which required tremendous strength after a heart attack. You have invested a lot of your time and energy into previous relationships which demonstrated your ability to commit to what is important to you. You have taken care of so many people; now it is time to invest in yourself. Commit to improving every aspect of your life. Improve your relationships, finances, communication skills, health, and your career.

Create a diversified investment portfolio where you are the relationship broker of your emotional stock market. The more you invest into yourself, the better the returns will be. The goal is to have higher stocks in assertiveness, confidence, respect and self-esteem and less stock in insecurity, jealousy, promiscuity and lies. Whatever is important to you will be represented in your emotional stock market. The bible says wherever your treasure is, your heart will be also (Matthew 6:21).

There is an important lesson for you to master here. You must learn that an emotionally immature man with character defects cannot afford you because you are priceless. Your stocks are high and the value of your assets are high. Do not allow a man to put you on lay-away to spend a little time with you and then leave you for a while until later on when he is ready for you. A man should not be able to borrow or loan you out. Require him to invest in your stocks and make regular deposits into you and the relationship. The man should also be required to keep his emotional stocks up as well because a woman cannot build his emotional portfolio for him. You can make emotional deposits into a man to support him and lift him up but you cannot change him, nor can you be his foundation. You can influence and inspire a man, but you cannot fix him. You have to be a gift to receive a gift and vice versa.

For example, Maggie told me that she didn't want to be in a committed relationship. She stated she liked to keep it simple. First of all, I knew she was lying because she was afraid of commitment and didn't want to open herself up to being hurt again. She was the ultimate female player. She had a collection of men to choose from any time she pleased. The problem was, her actions didn't match her words. She kept sending mixed messages to these guys. One minute she didn't want a relationship and the next minute she was upset because one of them didn't call her or was with another woman. Really!? It got to a point where I couldn't keep up so I told Maggie that until she gets serious about her own emotional stock market, no man was ever going to be serious about it for her. She was pimping and dishonoring herself.

Listen, my friend, you are so valuable and so worthy of the best. You are priceless. Once you respect yourself and start believing how beautiful and special you are, karma will honor you. God does not, nor has he ever made a mistake and you are not a mistake. Honor Him by building yourself up. A man who respects and loves you will want to invest in your stocks; he would be stupid not to. You are a queen. A queen knows her worth and honors it. She is regal, not conceited. She knows her self-worth and commands respect but she does not have an entitlement spirit. She is loyal, but not naively submissive. She is intelligent, independent, but not co-dependent. A queen honors her emotional boundaries from faith and not fear. A queen invests in her emotional stock market on a daily basis. She understands the power of her position.

Maggie struggled with reclaiming her power, releasing the pain and renewing her mind. Her worth was defined by the finer things in life such as her car, money, clothes, and her appearance. In reality, Maggie was bankrupt in her emotions, finances, relationships, and career.

For example, after Maggie opened up about her 51 sex partners, she decided she wanted to start counseling with me. At the time, I did not know that she suffered from stress and anxiety. This young lady had it all, so it appeared. I would honestly get excited to see her because I would learn about the latest fashion just from looking at her attire. I knew what was hot just by the shoes she wore or the purses she carried. This girl was fly! Not a strand of hair was out of place, her make-up was flawless, the car was tight and she rocked her lifestyle like it was the runway. She had it going on except the poor thing was stressed as hell. Why? Because she had no self-control and she did not understand the power of her position as a Queen.

Maggie worked hard Monday through Friday and when she got paid she bought what she wanted, went where she wanted, ate what she wanted and did just what she wanted to do all because she was trying to cover up her insecurities. Money had power over her.

As a child, she did not have a lot. Her family struggled and she vowed to never struggle again. The stress from the hustle was catching up to her. The check book was not balanced, instead the account was overdrawn and so was she. This young woman needed to repair and prepare her finances. It wasn't like she had a six figure salary, but she earned enough money to support herself. She lived above her means, which caused her to live paycheck-to-paycheck. Maggie borrowed money from friends too much until no one wanted to help her out anymore. She was ruining those relationships because friends felt like they were the ones giving and never receiving. Maggie blamed her job as the problem. She asserted that if her job paid her more she would be okay. She also complained about her co-workers and supervisor. Maggie believed everyone was against her and she was the victim.

After a few weeks of hearing all I could take, it was time for an intervention. I met Maggie at the front door when she came in for her next session. I locked the door behind me and stood directly in front of her staring into her eyes and I said, "You came to me because you said you needed help and you chose me to help you. Well today I am going to help you but you must surrender your fears right here at the door. Don't take another step if you don't trust me." I could see her eyes get bigger but I knew she was desperate for relief in her life and also curious of what I would do. She agreed by saying, "Okay." I instructed her to empty her purse on the floor and give it to me and she did it. I then told her to take off her jewelry and place it on the floor with her belongings and she did. Next, I handed her a pack of make-up remover towels and requested that she take her make-up off. She hesitated. I instructed her that she had two choices-Fear or Faith. She removed her make-up, but I had to remind her that she forgot to take her eyelashes off. Once again, she hesitated and once again I reminded her of her two choices- Fear or Faith. After she removed the make-up, I looked her in the eyes again and said, "Take off your hair." Maggie said, "What? Why in the hell do you want me to do that?" Once again, I reminded her that she had two choices- Fear or Faith.

We stood there for at least ten minutes. She began to shift her weight from one foot to the other. She looked at the walls and then she looked at me. She glanced at the floor and then the lights. I could see her anxiety increasing. She didn't know where this was going; she only knew it didn't feel good to her. There I stood in front of her taking away all of her comfort from her and she did not like the way it felt. Little did she know that I was not taking anything away from her because I only made the requests and she made the decisions.

Slowly she reached up and place her hand on her head and pulled her lace front wig off. Finally, I could see her surrendering. I smiled at her and told her to leave her red bottom shoes at the door and follow me. We walked into the restroom where I placed her square in front of the mirror. She didn't look at herself. I asked her to introduce me to the woman in the mirror. Then she tearfully began to open her heart and tell me about the woman who was looking back at her. That woman was weak, hurting, insecure, afraid and hopeless. I asked her to tell me more about the woman who met me at the door. She stated the woman at the door was everything her true self is not. The woman at the door tries to be brave, popular, independent, strong, beautiful and smart.

I took her tube of red lipstick and began to write on the mirror, "I cheat on myself," "I stress myself out trying to cover my imperfections," "I am fake," "Don't trust me because I don't trust myself," "Don't believe me when I say I love you because I don't love myself," "I don't take care of myself," "I abuse and disrespect myself," "I pimp myself." She quickly turned to me and said, "I didn't say any of those things so why did you write that?" I told her that she did not verbally say them but that is exactly what she is saying by the way she lives her life because she lives in fear and she has no self-control.

The point of this is Maggie had to learn how her insecurities affected her life. There was nothing wrong with her clothes, purse, shoes, make-up or hair. Heck, I thought the girl was fly! It was how she was using those material items to make herself feel secure, good enough, smart and beautiful and it was affecting her finances, job, and stressing her out.

You see, sometimes you have to focus on the other relationships in your life not just your failed relationships with men.

There are so many other relationships to repair. In this case, Maggie had to repair the relationship with herself and money. The journey was long and difficult at times. Heck there were times when I wanted to break up with her but I stayed put because I understood the lesson she would learn in the end. It wasn't the basics of money management that she had to learn. It was about making her decisions from faith and not fear; not leaning irresponsibly on her bank account to make her feel good. Maggie's recovery period was very long. She easily identified her emotional boundaries, but she struggled with honoring them. Maggie knew her heart defects and started the healing process after releasing so much pain. She fought temptations daily; however the amount of emotional investment she gave to herself was priceless. I could see her fall in love with her true self. She began to change her relationship with money and she stretched her skills at work in the process.

Once she learned to look at her true self in the mirror and accept the insecure woman then she could begin to help the insecure woman prepare to become a secure woman. She learned that every night when she stepped out of her car and walked into her house, took off her clothes, hair and face she was sleeping with her true self. Each morning, she woke up with her true self and whenever she stepped out the door it was her true self that made decisions for her even though she looked like a different woman. This girl pimped herself until she was stressed and financially struggling. She had to make a decision about how long she would continue to disrespect and dishonor herself. How long she would cheat on herself and how long she would steal from herself. She was stealing money from herself. Nobody else was robbing her. The good news is she doesn't spend money out of fear anymore and she does not make her decisions out of fear. Before she had fear of not looking her best, fear of not having the best, fear of looking cheap or broke, and fear of being broke. Maggie knows how to invest in herself emotionally, hence the money doesn't have to take care of her emotionally.

Invest in your Relationships

I have had plenty of women to come into my office for counseling only to find out that they neglected some part of their lives whenever they were involved in a relationship with a man. I mentioned in the introduction of this book that when a woman loves, she loves hard and deeply. She is totally committed. There is nothing wrong with that unless there is an imbalance in your life. With that being said, the only relationship that I want to encourage you to focus on right now is the relationship with yourself. Fall in love with you and get to know yourself all over again. As you live life you change. That is what life does to us, it changes us either good or bad. Look at yourself and nobody else. Ask yourself why do you hang around the people you hang around? Why do you do the things you do? Really start looking inward and piecing the puzzle together.

In a previous chapter, I encouraged you to choose your weapon to resist temptations because, believe me, it's coming. Use this recovery time to do you. If you are in college, read more and get ahead on the syllabus for your classes or get involved in new activities to meet new people. At work, step out of your comfort zone and believe in yourself by volunteering to work on a new project to highlight your skills and strengths. Whatever you do, just focus on you. In the meantime, there may be a few relationships you will need to invest more time in such as friends and family members. Then again, there are some relationships or friendships you will have to let go of.

Even though I am encouraging you to focus on yourself, there are times when focusing on yourself too much can become an issue. When a woman says she does not want a relationship because she is focusing on her career, it's the truth. On the contrary, when a man says he is not ready for a relationship it means he is not ready to settle down with one woman. Many women have chosen to focus on their career and have put relationships or friendships on hold. The problems start once a woman pulls her head up out of the sand and realize she is alone. Afterwards, it can be difficult for her to have the relationship she wants because she has been disconnected for so long or the caliber of men don't measure up.

My friend, you must have balance in your life. Time will not and has never waited on anyone or anything. The days, months and years will go by and you will be in a situation of playing catch up. Do not sabotage your life like that. An emotionally healthy and happy person has balance in relationships and in their career. Find a way to have balance because it equals happiness.

Invest in Your Finances

Some people say money is the root of all evil but I disagree. It is the character of the person and their relationship with money that can be an issue. Sadly, a woman with money issues is like a ship without an oar. She is not grounded, stable or secure. You must not depend on a man to provide your financial security because you have no control in that. This is the time to learn how to make your money, manage your money, invest and grow your money. I had to learn that money is an energy, meaning I had to demote it from the CEO of my life to customer service. My advice to you is do not chase money and do not worry about money because those actions give too much power to it. Do not allow anything or anyone to have power over you like that.

Money can destroy relationships and it will make some women do some desperate, irresponsible and risky things. Step back, my friend, and take a hard look at your bank account. If you do not have a checking or savings account then get one. Honor yourself by being in control of your financial future. Invest in your retirement and 401(k) plans. Spending money on $400 hair weave, $40 on gel manicures and pedicures, $250 on drinks at the club, and $1,000 on clothes adds up to a nice amount to invest. Look at what you are spending your money on because that, too, has power over you. You consume what is important to you and whatever is important to you can take on the role of god in your life.

Invest in your Career

If you have a job say, "Hallelujah!" If you have a career and you love it, say "Thank you Jesus." That's right, many folks don't have a job and there are some with jobs and they don't love it. How about this…start doing what you love; don't settle. You see, once again you have to focus on a relationship and it's you. I keep giving you the same message for a reason. Do not settle for any man and do not settle for just any career. If you are in a job you do not like, guess what? You will complain about it and the people around you will get tired of you complaining about your job. Heck, the man in your life will too.

This reminds me of a lady in her forties who had severe depression, but it was situational depression. Situational depression basically means she was depressed because of the situations in her life not because it was clinical depression. She was unhappy about being overweight, complained about her job and the people who worked there, she was unhappy in her marriage, and she moped around about not having friends. Heck, this lady was depressed about her whole life; it was difficult to get her to see the blessings she had. Unfortunately, she was comfortable being depressed and comfortable with complaining; however she was uncomfortable with change and growth. Why? Because it required her to focus on herself, stop pointing the finger at others, and work hard. She didn't have the energy or passion to fight for herself and no one else could do it for her.

When a woman is in need, at some point a man will try to fix her problems only to find out that he cannot fix job problems. Sometimes women do not want men to fix their problems they just want men to listen. The good news is your career problems can be fixed by you. It is time to take a career inventory of your strengths, skills, interests, challenges and resources. What makes you happy; is it the money or the job? Do not get me wrong, I know you need to make a decent salary to survive and thrive; however you must be happy and content with the job you choose and work hard for the job you want. Ask yourself if you need to go back to school or get an additional certification? Do you need to meet with a professional who can help you update your resume? Are you involved and connected within your profession? Look at the resources that are around you and see which ones you can tap into such as networking groups, Chamber of Commerce meetings, professional groups, or civic meetings. I don't want you to just be happy in your relationships, I want you to be happy in all areas of your life and it takes time and hard work. Think about it. Relationships, finances, career and health all affect one another. If you are happy with your career but having relationship issues it can affect your work performance because stress does not discriminate. Consequently, if you are having financial problems it may affect your mental and emotional health.

Now if for some reason you do not feel motivated to hustle for your career then you have to strip down to the roots to get to the deeper issues. You have two choices- Fear or Faith.

Invest in your Health

I am not the healthiest person in the world but I definitely believe in self-care. At the beginning of a New Year, some people make weight loss resolutions that they abandon within three months. I want to encourage you to live a healthy lifestyle every day. Be healthy emotionally, mentally, physically and spiritually. That is all I want for you. Look at each area and ask yourself, "How emotionally fit am I?" "Am I physically healthy?" "What do I need to do to get spiritually fit?"

Do you think a good man wants to be in a relationship with a woman who is not emotionally healthy? Physically healthy? Mentally healthy? What about spiritually healthy? You have to be a gift to receive a gift. This process is about you being your best and taking the time to prepare. Remember the recovery period does not have a time constraint; it varies for each individual. Take another inventory to see if you are cheating on yourself or disrespecting yourself when it comes to your health. Visit you doctor regularly for wellness check-ups, take care of your teeth; don't skip flossing because it can help decrease your risk of heart problems. Occasionally, treat yourself to a massage or facial and do not be afraid to see a Therapist if you need to. Take the time to pray and meditate because it can help with stress reduction and improve your mood. One last thing; exercise.

What excuses are you making that are keeping you from spiritual or physical health? Believe it or not but your health also is connected to your overall self-esteem and confidence. Do it for yourself because a man cannot do it for you. Remember, you are what you consume; garbage in will equal garbage out.

Virtuous Woman Blueprint

The concepts I have provided in this book are simple, yet difficult to do. It requires a lot of introspection, internal pruning and discipline. Increasing your emotional stock market can best be learned from a woman who is an expert in building up her worth. The virtuous woman, in the bible, is the elite female role model for a woman who desires to transform who she is. The book of Proverbs is a compilation of the wisdom of King Solomon. When Solomon was made King, God asked him what he wanted and he asked God to give him wisdom. In some biblical interpretations, it may say that Solomon asked for an understanding heart. Nevertheless, the book of Proverbs offers insightful wisdom to apply in your life today.

In chapter 31, which is the last chapter of the book, the virtuous woman is introduced and described. I encourage you to slowly read the entire chapter. Dissect each verse and ask yourself how you can be a virtuous woman. She is an extraordinary woman of worth, determination, love, strength, and kindness. My favorite verse is number 25, which says, "Strength and dignity are her clothing, and she smiles at the future." She embraces and wraps herself in her strength and self-worth. She knows that she is priceless; and she knows that she is respected. The virtuous woman is described as a good homemaker, business woman, hard worker, giving, prepared, hopeful, happy, and wise. It sounds like her emotional stock market is diversified and providing good earnings and returns. I challenge you to increase your emotional stocks. I double dare you! Who do you love more, that man or yourself?

Use the chart below to write what is important to you in each area.

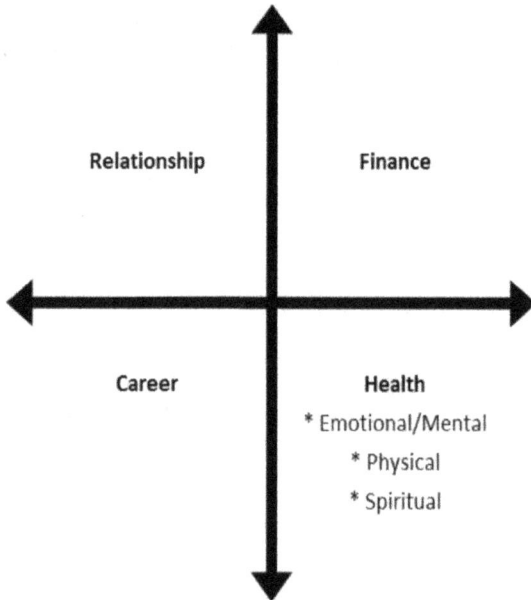

Relationship

Finance

Career

Health
* Emotional/Mental
* Physical
* Spiritual

Heart Notes

♥ What relationships are important to you?

♥ What positive investments do these relationships need?

♥ Are you able to make the investments into these relationships?

♥ How will improving these relationships increase your emotional stocks?

♥ What type of relationship do you have with money?

♥ Are you making money decisions out of fear or faith?

♥ What positive investments are needed to improve your finances?

♥ What do you need to do to improve your physical health? Emotional health? Spiritual health?

♥ Have you been complaining about your job?

♥ What investments do you need to make in your career?

♥ How will improving your finances and health increase your emotional stock?

♥ The goals for your career are_____.

♥ The goals for your physical health are____.

♥ The goals for your emotional health are____.

♥ The goals for your spiritual health are____.

♥ Your purpose in life is____.

♥ If God asked you, "What do you want?" what would you ask Him for?

Scriptures

He who loves money will not be satisfied with money, nor he who loves abundance with its income. This too is vanity. Ecclesiastes 5:10

The Lord is my shepherd, I shall not want...surely goodness and loving kindness will follow me all the days of my life. Psalm 23:1, 6

For I know the plans that I have for you, declares the Lord, plans for welfare and not for calamity to give you a future and hope. Jeremiah 29:11

11
A GOOD THING

It is true. A good man is hard to find. I am dead serious because I would not even know where to start looking for a good man. I have heard people say go to church, the grocery store or the gym. Heck, bad men hang out in those places too. My advice to women is to stop looking because women were not designed to be hunters. Men, on the other hand, were created to go out and hunt and bring back the food. It's not that women cannot take care of themselves, but men have an innate instinct to be providers and protectors. This doesn't mean all men are good at it, but the ability is within them. If you want to be in a serious, committed, loving relationship you do not have to go out looking for a man.

On the other hand, there is a man I would suggest you pursue or chase for the time being. He desperately wants to be in a serious relationship with you; his name is God. He is also the best heart surgeon in the world. God wants an emotionally intimate relationship with you and you do not have to worry about Him being emotionally immature. He says you can trust him because he will not leave you, hurt you or forget about you. God is really into you as he already knows the depths of your heart, the number of hairs on your head and what you are thinking. He will support you and love you as well as be patient with you. He is waiting for you to trust and open your heart to him. If you have any unresolved Daddy issues, then God will be a Father to you. Nevertheless, He is very open about being involved with other women because he has the power to give women the desires of their heart.

As you spend more time with God and the more serious your relationship becomes with Him, he will encourage you to take it to the next level by proving his love and commitment to you. He just wants you to give Him a chance. Heck, He has been asking you out for a while now (knocking at your heart). If you give him a try, you will experience a love and intimacy like you have never felt before and you will want more of Him. As you abide with Him, He will reveal the plan for your life and bring you to your partner just like he brought Eve to Adam. You will not have to look for a man because your partner will find you. As you recognize, honor and accept the beautiful mind, loving heart, gracious soul and fabulous spirit that you are God will present you as a beloved and sacred gift to a man who will also be a beloved and sacred gift to you.

Take a step back and look at the snapshot. Men do not grow up playing house and dreaming about being the knight in shining armor to their princess. Women are the ones who played house as little girls and dreamed of a fairytale world. So basically men explore, play, build, tear down, collect, redevelop, and then decide to settle down.

In the beginning, God created heaven and earth. He created man in His own image and gave man authority over the earth and the creatures within it. After God created Adam, he saw that Adam was alone in the Garden of Eden. It was then that God stated Adam needed a suitable partner. At that time, God performed the first major surgery in history using a rib from Adam to create Eve. God could have taken a bone from any part of Adam's body; instead he decided to use the bone closest to Adam's heart to create a woman. After Eve was created, God took her and presented her to Adam. Never did Eve have to go searching for the man as God brought the two together.

The scripture says, "He who finds a wife finds a good thing and obtains favor from the Lord" (Proverbs 18:22). I guess that means there is a man somewhere in this world looking for his wife. In counseling, I have had the privilege of many men opening their hearts to me. I have learned that when a man is ready to settle down, he starts looking for his mate. There are some men who aren't looking just yet and they luckily meet an awesome woman with her stuff together. He then realizes that he would be foolish to let her go. Men like a woman who is already upgraded. They are attracted to women whose emotional stock market is healthy and diversified. They recognize her emotional wealth and value and want to invest in her. If you are forcing or rushing a man to put a ring on your finger, STOP! Don't push, manipulate, threaten, or rush him.

If marriage is what you want, then you have to start demonstrating you are ready for the sacred covenant of marriage. What I mean is go back to the basics of honor, trust, support, patience and respect. Deal with your root issues. Rest, reflect and prepare yourself because a man who finds a wife finds a good thing and you have to be a good thing when you meet him.

Once you meet the man for you put the physical intimacy on the back porch. Keep honor and respect in the center of your relationship. Be aware of your emotional boundaries, do not compromise on the character and values, communicate from your heart, and focus on the emotional intimacy. A woman who has undergone reconstructive heart surgery and dealt with her heart defects is a gift. You are a gift, my friend. And just like the wise men who brought gifts to the newborn Savior, you will receive a gift as well. Prepare yourself to receive it and be blessed.

S.W.A.G.

Sometimes single women look at my relationship that I have now and want to know how they can have the same thing. I am not perfect; I have had my heart broken a few times and I know what it is like to reclaim your power, release the pain and renew your mind. I have been there and done that.

During my recovery period, I was focused on my S.W.A.G. It is not the type of swag the popular world may think it is. Instead, it's the Single Woman and God kind of swag. I spent a lot of time flirting with God and long nights talking to him. We had intimate talks when I prayed and I just adored him; God and I became really close. At the throne, I learned how to be patient, how to be accountable for my actions and decisions, and most importantly, I learned my purpose. Overall, the lesson that I had to master in my relationship with God was to listen to Him, obey Him, trust Him, serve Him, and love Him. That is all He wants from you too. All I know is once my heart healed and I was focused on investing in myself, a good man found me. I didn't look for him; he found me. God decided it was time for me to have a man in my life and He presented me to him.

It was a summer day after the 7:45 am church service at New Beginning Full Gospel Baptist Church. My girlfriend and I went to Lenox Mall in Atlanta to do some shopping. We were discussing our disappointments in the young men wearing their pants hanging off their butts. Unfortunately, the best pick-up line most of those men had was, "What's up, Shorty?"

After being in the mall long enough, we decided it was time for us to leave. While walking through Macy's I saw a handsome gentleman in a suit walking towards us. He had his Barack Obama strut going on, he appeared confident, and he was minding his own business. No agenda. I looked at him and kindly said, "You look nice in your suit." I honestly wanted to give the brother a compliment after seeing so many knuckle heads in the mall holding their pants up with one hand while trying to walk.

The gentleman smiled and said, "Thank you" and we both kept walking in separate directions; however he decided to turn around and stop me. He asked for my number and I said, "No" because I was enjoying my recovery period and didn't feel the need to get involved with anyone. Long story short, after much encouragement from my girlfriend, we exchanged phone numbers and had long conversations on a regular basis. We both focused on ourselves during the week and we saw each other on the weekend and did fun activities together.

I had learned a lot from previous heart attacks so I had to see if this guy was worth putting on my V.I.P. list. I had to see if he had the character and values that were important to me. I made sure to do things differently with this man and I knew that I only had two choices- fear or faith. I communicated my emotional boundaries with him and watched carefully for any red flags except I didn't see any red flags. Everything was perfect; no games and no drama. Every now and then, I would ask God when the wolf was going to show up because it was too good to be true. At least that is what I thought.

Later in our friendship, I provided him with a journal to share with me so that I could get to know him better. I called it a couples' journal. He would keep the journal for a week and write in it and I would read it on the weekend and keep the journal with me for a week and write in it. The journal went back and forth between his house and mine. We learned so much about each other. I learned more about what he did at work, his stressors, his goals, his sense of humor, and his character. We learned how to open up to each other. We also learned how to communicate from the heart.

In the end, God rewarded me for my obedience. One year after meeting that gentlemen he proposed to me and eleven months after the proposal we were married. He was consistent with the four principles of a healthy relationship- trust, support, patience and respect. He communicated well and compromised when it was necessary. It was not difficult to love this man; nothing was hard about the union. Eleven years later, we are still loving each other. I say all of this because even though you may be hurting now or getting over a heart break, joy will come in the morning. Each day you show God what is important to you and who is important to you by how you spend your time and what you consume. Will it be four to five hours of reality television or a few hours with God? Will it be texting, Facebook, Twitter, Instagram or God? Make a decision. In the meantime, I suggest you get your S.W.A.G. on with God; be patient and wait on the Lord.

I love You

When you meet the right man and fall in love with him, it only makes sense that at some point you will want to say, "I love you" to him. It is okay if you do, but it must be at the right time. If you say it too soon then the guy may feel obligated to say it back to you even if he is not ready or he may shut down. You don't want that to happen.

First, you must consider what you are really saying when you say, 'I love you.' Women let it roll off their tongues to show how much they care, but there is more in the phrase than those three simple words. 'I love you' means you appreciate him, you admire him, and respect him. It also means you accept him and have chosen him to be a part of your life. 'I love you' also means he is right for you at that moment in your life and you want to build on what you have with him. You are saying you love his character and his values. Basically, you are communicating that you want to keep him.

In the beginning of a new relationship, if you feel the urge to blurt out, "I love you" replace it with, "I like…" Tell your new partner what you like about him. There are five basic needs of a man: admiration and respect, domestic, recreational, attractive wife, and sex. Start out by telling him how much (and why) you admire and respect him. By the time you say, "I love you," it will feel really good to his ears, but most importantly his heart.

Pepe´ La Pew Syndrome

When I was a little girl, I loved the Looney Tunes character, Pepe´ La Pew. He was a French skunk with a terrible odor and a determination to be in love. Ironically, he was in love with a black cat, except he didn't know she was a cat. The cat had mistakenly bumped into a ladder and a can of white paint fell onto her back and she ended up with a white stripe.

Pepe´ would chase the cat to proclaim his love for her. Whenever he caught her, he would shower her with affectionate kisses. He never gave up and he never got the message that she was not interested. She would scratch him and do everything in her power to run away. Pepe´ smothered the heck out of the one he loved, but it is not necessary for you to do that. When you meet a good man, step back and breathe deeply. Remember all the hard work you did to reclaim your power and release the pain. You are a Queen and you have the most powerful position.

Men and women naturally need independence in a relationship. What I mean is, it is important to have your identity and the free-will to continue doing the fun, respectable things you enjoyed prior to meeting one another. Do not be afraid to honor his Sunday afternoon basketball games at the gym or his Saturday golf time. You wouldn't want him restraining you from your Wednesday night bible study, hair stylist or cocktail dates with your friends. 'Trust' is not the enemy. It's the man's character that reveals you cannot trust him, but that does not mean you stop trusting people. The art of loving and the art of trusting is a beautiful thing. Let him know you are interested in him, but there is no need to hand cuff him to the wall because he will run away if you do.

When my husband and I were dating, we really enjoyed each other's time. One night he called me up and asked me what I had planned for the weekend because he wanted to hang out. I nicely told him that I had plans. He asked me what would I be doing and I told him, "Just chilling and relaxing." He was shocked! Later on he told me that he appreciated that I had my own life and he was happy to see I didn't need to be around him all the time. In other words, we both didn't want to be smothered.

Do not be afraid of space because it can be a priceless moment for reflection while you are dating. It also helps you not to move too quickly, especially if your heart is moving faster than your brain.

The Covenant

A few times in this book I mentioned stories of young ladies who had been "playing house." They lived with the man, cooked, cleaned, washed clothes, had sex, paid bills, and broke up. When it comes to playing house, I am like Homey the clown, a straight-forward clown played by Damon Wayans on the show, *In Living Color*, "Homey don't play that."

This is my opinion, but write this down anyway, "Do not play house or wife with a single man." Would you start a clothing boutique and give all of the clothes in the store away for free? Of course you wouldn't. So do not give your worth, time, talents, and gifts away for free. You need a commitment before you do that and the only commitment that I am talking about is marriage. An engagement ring is not the commitment; it is a symbol of the expected commitment. There are many people who break off their engagement. The covenant is what seals the commitment. The covenant is the agreement or the vows that you and your partner make to one another. The covenant is very sacred. It is signed, sealed and delivered on the wedding day. Playing house is not the commitment or the covenant.

Is it the glam of a wedding that you want or the covenant? Do you want the diamond ring to bling in front of your friends or the covenant? Do you want to play house with him or do you want him to buy you a house? Do you want to pay bills with him or build wealth together? You have to understand what you are asking for. The covenant is not for a few months; the covenant is for a lifetime. Heck, society has already seen people spend millions of dollars on a wedding only to have the marriage last no more than 90 days. The covenant is a serious matter and it should not be entered into lightly.

Build the right foundation in future relationships. Use the hierarchy relationship chart, as a reference.

Hierarchy of Relationship Needs

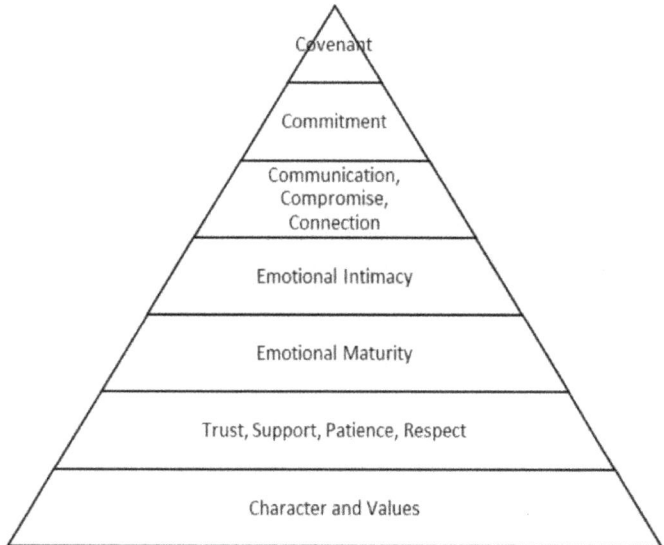

Covenant

Commitment

Communication,
Compromise,
Connection

Emotional Intimacy

Emotional Maturity

Trust, Support, Patience, Respect

Character and Values

Heart Notes

♥ What little gods in your life has replaced God?

♥ How much of your time do you give to God?

♥ What does your behavior communicate about your relationship with God?

♥ Do you believe there is no perfect place to meet a man and that you can meet a man anywhere?

♥ It is not the meeting place that is important, it is what you do when you see him such as: smile, say "hello", make eye contact, etc.

♥ Each new relationship will test your strength and values to see if you have mastered the previous lessons.

♥ Do not be afraid to trust; do not be afraid to love.

♥ Resist the Pepe´ La Pew syndrome. Give each other necessary space when needed.

♥ What does marriage mean to you?

Scriptures

But the fruit of the Spirit is love, joy, peace, patience, kindness, goodness, faithfulness, gentleness, self-control; against such things there is no law. Galatians 5:22, 23

But from there you will seek the Lord, your God, and you will find Him if you search for Him with all your heart and all your soul. Deuteronomy 4:29

He who finds a wife finds a good thing and obtains favor from the Lord" Proverbs 18:22

But now faith, hope, love, abide these three; but the greatest of these is love. 1 Corinthians 13:13

TEN COMMANDMENTS OF A WOMAN'S HEART

- ♥ Thou shall love, serve and trust God.
- ♥ Thou shall not lie.
- ♥ Thou shall love, honor and respect yourself.
- ♥ Thou shall let go.
- ♥ Thou shall open up.
- ♥ Thou shall listen.
- ♥ Thou shall have faith.
- ♥ Thou shall grow.
- ♥ Thou shall love others.
- ♥ Thou shall inspire, encourage and empower.

CHARTS

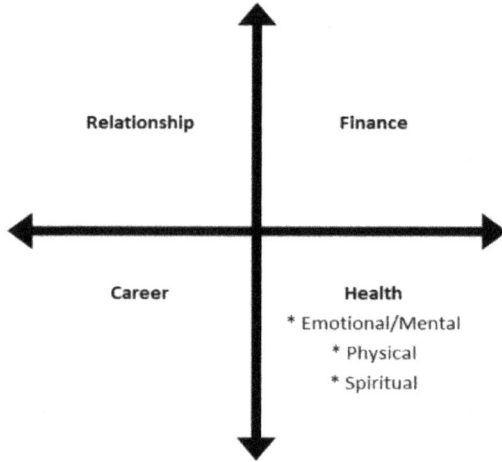

Relationship   Finance

Career   Health
* Emotional/Mental
* Physical
* Spiritual

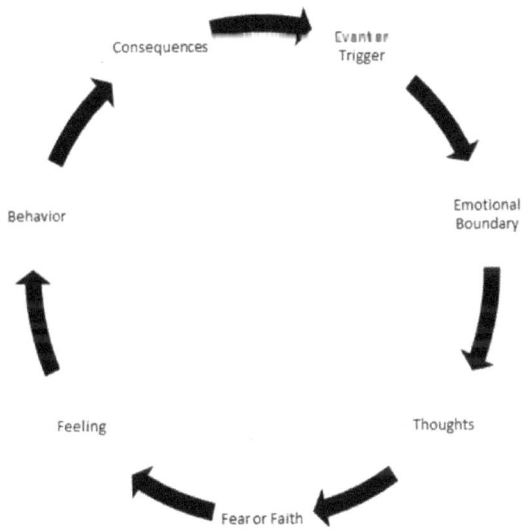

Hierarchy of Relationship Needs

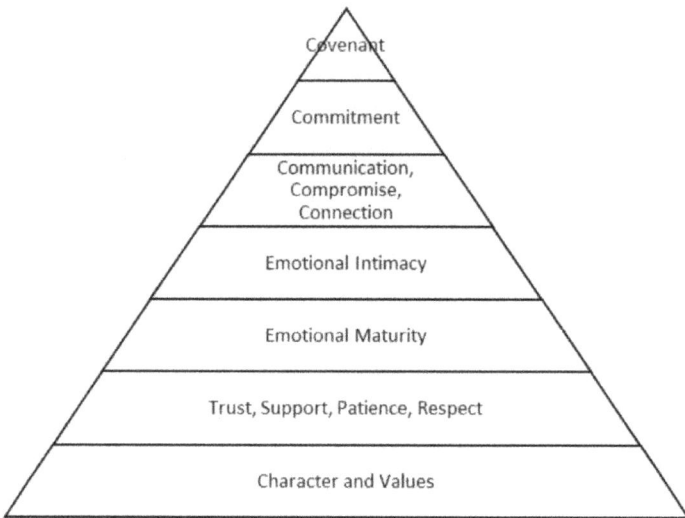

Covenant

Commitment

Communication,
Compromise,
Connection

Emotional Intimacy

Emotional Maturity

Trust, Support, Patience, Respect

Character and Values

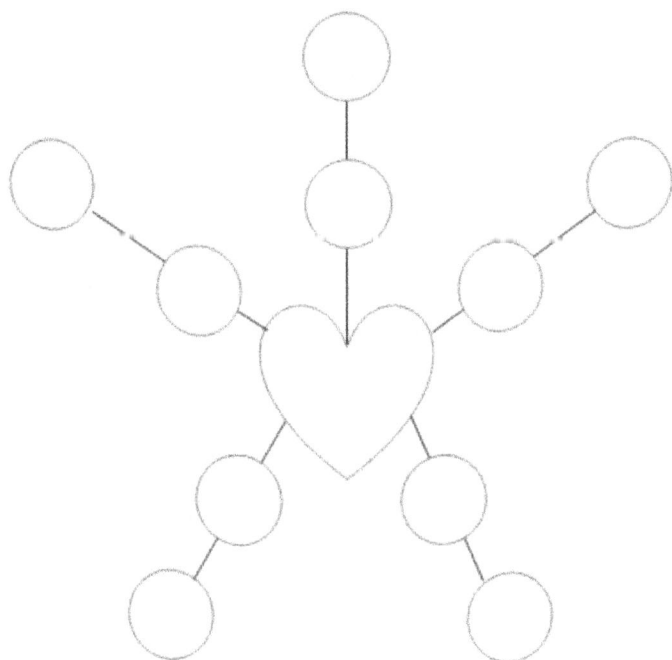

ABOUT AUTHOR

Shaneka McClarty is a licensed therapist, consultant, and speaker. She speaks frequently to church women's groups, conferences, and non-profit organizations. Shaneka received her Bachelor's Degree from Stillman College (Tuscaloosa, AL) and her Masters of Arts degree from Argosy University (Atlanta, GA). She lives in Tucker, GA with her husband, Leonardo, and their three daughters, Sage, Sydney and Sarai.

To book Shaneka for speaking engagements or counseling sessions, visit her website at www.therapygirl.net.

9 780615 962788